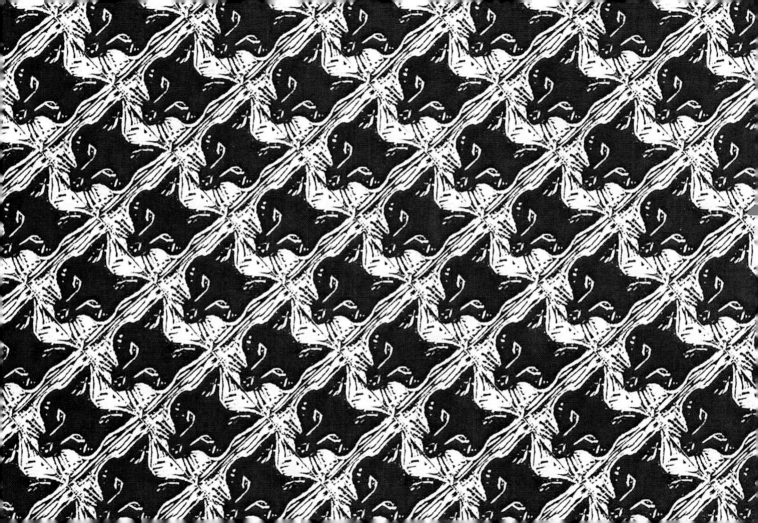

England! England

Published by Urban Fox Press
www.urbanfoxpress.com

First published 2006

Urban Fox Press,
6 Albert Road,
Chatham, Kent,
ME4 5PZ,
England

Printed in Kent, England
ISBN 1-905522-16-9
978-1-905522-16-3

England! England

A Pinhole View Of The South: Part 1

urbanfoxpress.chatham

England! England
Now that the Gods have left us,
What?

5 pm. Saturday 9th June, 2006.

Maidstone High Street; a spitting, swaying, scrapping flag of St George. Isolated pockets of frightened mothers shepherd children away from urinating Arians into the relative safety of McDonalds and Blockbusters. The police allow themselves to be beaten back with nothing fiercer than volleys of 'Tomorrow belongs to me' and slink away quietly, perhaps hoping that this fury dies out of its own accord. They could make arrests, but who to stick the cuffs on? There aren't enough cuffs, enough police vans, enough cells, enough officers who believe in anything other than easy targets and easy overtime…

It's like this every time the England football team play.
England! England!

Behind me a bottle smashes. A large group, some fifteen young men, all sporting England football shirts, are having fun. I keep walking. There's no point in making a fuss. They're young, let them throw bottles. And let us old men walk away. Unfortunately my friend thinks otherwise.

I turn to see him surrounded and taking punches from numerous fists. I have little choice but to go to his aid.

"Hang on," I say, "this isn't fair, let him fight one on one." I don't want to split up the fight. My friend was stupid enough to get himself into this – who's to say he didn't bring it on himself? - and he can get himself out. But fifteen onto one? Is this right?

England! England.

"Ok," a lad in a baseball cap agrees, backing away, "fair enough." I turn to watch my friend, hoping he won't get beaten too badly. Immediately the gang drag me to the ground and begin kicking. What a fool I am, I think as I curl up - trying to lessen the damage - a real life Don Quioxte. So naïve to think that honour exists here, in the heart of this grey and putrefying land. My immune system closes my brain down. I remember nothing more. Until I'm standing up, facing them once again, and the baseball cap is screaming,

"Come on, come on!" I just stare because I don't feel that I can do anything else. The gang turn and run.

My ribs ache. I shoulder my friend for a mile up to the 'Dog and Gun' and hand him over to his wife. Another fight breaks out before I leave the pub. A young man is punched. The attack is unprovoked. The crunch of his head smacking the floor sickens me. His girlfriend screams.

"I'm pregnant, he's going to be a father, leave him alone…" I don't know the lad but I step in to make the peace, imploring others in the pub to help me. I don't do this because I'm a saint or a particularly good bloke even. But if we don't care for each other, what else is there? How can our society, our world, function? Old men look on blankly and young men pretending to be old huff melodramatically

"We're just out for a quiet night, we don't want no trouble," they ignore the man on the floor, who lies deathly still, and the red faced aggressor, and turn on me, "just fuck off now, we don't want no trouble."

My Granddad used to rule the roost in this pub. And his father before him. It was their local. Both my parents lived five minutes walk away as kids. Is this what they prayed was in store for their descendents? Did the old men fight on the Somme, in Tripoli, Sicily and Berlin, to defend their neighbours right to act so cowardly? I doubt they actually considered it, amongst all the hell of day to day living back then, but if they did…did they really hope to give birth to a nation that can proudly face up to an Islamic enemy raised by the media (as long as they have powerful guns and numbers behind them) yet which turns on the weakest link when the call goes out to moral men to stand up for goodness, against the odds, in their own backyard?

England. England.

Maybe my recent beating has knocked the rose-tinted glasses off, perhaps it was always like this here, and I couldn't see it because I'm among it. We have everything, in this country, we want for nothing, and yet…this is how it is.

At home I can't lie down. An excruciating pain stabbing at my left side and shoulder keeps me propped upright. I stare into darkness, relieving my past, the many journeys made on foot through hundreds of miles of rural Africa and the Middle East, trying to remember a time when I might've encountered a group of humans with such a noticeable lack of empathy for their fellow man as those I've met tonight have. But there're no such memories. Without a doubt, the tribes of North Kent are the most savage I've come across in the entire world…

I think about taking a trip to the emergency department but…what is this the result of if not a fight between yobs? We're no better than one another. I can't even remember who started it. I didn't see. It wasn't me, but my friend? I believe not, but I can't be sure. I won't waste the hospitals time. I'll just sit it out. It's probably just a broken rib anyhow.

Five days later, the pain subsides, I feel that I'm recovering well. Then, a sunny morning, I forget to take a hay fever tablet...

I sneeze as I drive, there's a sharp pain in my left side, and gradually the world grows misty and cold. I pull over into a farmer's field, feel the corn crunch under the wheels. Rows of elegant silver-green poplar trees crowning the horizon sway and bend and disappear. Inside two minutes I'm staring wide eyed at a blank white screen.

"Is this how it is for blind people?" I think, "is this how they live their whole life?"

I lay in the car, seat reclined, window down, for two hours that seem like ten minutes. My jeans and shirt are drenched, literally sopping, with sweat. I don't know it but the sneeze has ruptured my spleen, which has been weakened by a few well placed kicks, and I'm in shock, slowly bleeding to death from the inside out, my senses – sight, hearing, touch – closing down one by one. I drink a litre of cranberry juice, tear off some ham – I was on my way for a picnic – and try to wait it out. It never occurs to me that I might not get out of this situation. That these birds I hear in the rustling trees, their call fading with the minutes, might be the last sounds to grace my ears.

The pendulum swings. The space between life and death, the point of influence that tips us one way or the other, both are so minute, so discreet. If there's a thought that inspires me back from the brink, perhaps a memory of somebody I want to see again, or a place, a taste, a feeling or, if I believed in such things, an angel in the car beside me, if there's something, it's forgotten immediately after it does its job. I don't know why I live because in this situation most people don't. But I do.

I regain a little vision, feel the breeze, sit upright and drive to hospital. There's one nearby but I want to get back to Medway, two hours away, so that if I have to stay in I'm close to my family. I don't want to cause them the trouble of having to travel far to visit me.

I crunch up my stomach, hunch over the wheel – it's more comfortable that way, the spleen is so swollen it feels like an orange stuck up the back of my shirt - and concentrate. I stare at the white line in the middle of the road. Keep my thoughts together. Tell myself that this is all about mind over matter. About not letting the body dictate what I can and can't do.

I park up at Medway Maritime Hospital, walk doubled over to emergency, and politely give my details. Perhaps too politely. There's no rush to have me seen. When I'm eventually called through I can't lie down on the examination bench. My stomach is full to bursting with leaked blood.

"Try," the nurse says.

"I can't." He looks at me witheringly, as if I'm putting it on. He prods my belly as I lean back on my arms.

"Does this hurt?"

"Yes," I say, trying not to yelp. He prods again. Everywhere he touches is pain. I wince. My feet rise from the bench involuntarily.

"Rate the pain on a scale of one to ten," he says.

"Seven?" I reply, not wanting to be a wimp. How can you answer that question? He asks again. I remember friends in Africa. What's my pain compared to their everyday life? How can I complain?

"Eight?" I try again. He nods and leaves, not really believing I'm very ill, I think. I start to sweat, and the world spins as though I've drunk far too much, which I haven't, not a drop, and since I can't lie down I lean forward, bracing myself with my arms.

"Can you stand?" I'm staring at a pool of scarlet blood. "Can you hear me? Can you stand?" I can't understand who's talking or what they mean. Two male nurses haul me to my feet. "You feinted," one says. I've a gash in my head where I've nose-dived off the bench and head butted the wall, a smashed nose and a neck that, having taken the full force of my body, feels fractured.

I hope that now perhaps they'll believe I'm ill and help me. I'm sent for an X-ray. Afterwards I sit in the corridor waiting for the results. My face is caked in blood, my head wound weeps, I've no shirt on and my stomach's swollen, full of puddles of blood and wind. Passers-by stare and register 'hooligan' in their expression. Police officers linger in the hallway, suspiciously. The registrar studies my X-ray and announces that I've nothing seriously wrong, just a broken rib. He wants to send me home. Luckily a relative of mine is working the night shift in casualty, and is a better nurse than the guy in charge.

"He's not going home," she says, "pain in the left shoulder, it's obvious, he's got internal bleeding. He's staying in."

There's much murmuring and sobbing in the observation ward. The sound of sick people falling to sleep. Cleaners, guided by the half light of reception, swab the floor, sticking their finger in the dyke against a tide of MRSA. Blood mingles with salt water in the tube fixed to my arm. It looks like a strawberry slush puppy. My neck screams from where it broke my fall. The others in the ward get morphine. I get paracetamol. I'm a self inflicted wound, I think, they think. On the days when the England football team play, which was when I got attacked but also tonight, hospital casualty admissions go up from thirty on average to one hundred at least.

England. England.

Litanies of unfortunate people are wheeled past. Old men who, as soon as they're tucked up, get out of bed and shuffle towards the door like homing pigeons. When they're challenged they look at the nurse blankly and allow themselves to be helped back to bed for a few minutes, until the cycle repeats itself. An old woman cries

"What about the people under my bed! When are you going to make them leave?"

At midday my head is cleaned up (the blood, now dried, needs scrubbing, and the wound re-opens under the force of the scouring pad) and I'm moved to McCullock Ward. The five other patients in my room chat erratically, offering fearful glances left, right and behind, running from death, using conversation as a ruse to get their life stories told, which are average at best, and equally best forgotten by anybody who hasn't had the misfortune to live them. I think this because I hate them and I hate them because I know nothing and blame them for it because there's nobody else to blame. I want to rip this transfusion set from my arm and smash them all with it. Then I take my drugs and nothing matters.

Word gets round that I'm not a football yob. That I'm here after being attacked and that, as far as 2006 perception goes, my injuries aren't my fault. Nurses begin to smile. The registrar who was going to send me home peeps around the door and gives an embarrassed wave. My fellow patients, the ones who can talk (Tom can't, just lies there staring, unblinking), Navy Laurie (spinal cancer), Blonde Amazon Karen (stomach tumour), Uncle John (bladder problem) and Old Reg (ninety two and just wearing out) are keen to relieve their boredom by learning the new boys' story.

"Do you hate the blokes who did this to you?' John asks after I spill the news. I don't care enough about them to hate them, I think, I'll leave the hate to those that feel (their parents), as befits a man with nowhere to hang his rage and an eye on his peers' admiration.

"Don't know really," I shrug. "Haven't thought about them too much till now."

Then John's newborn is brought in, and I'm yesterday's news as we crowd around, staring at the wonder of life, and hovering, waiting, for its first lie and promise of salvation.

I'm woken hourly. The nurses want to check I'm still alive. I'm aggrieved but strangely satisfied. I like the attention that this illness brings me, the drama of being in a life or death situation. At any moment, they say, I could haemorrhage. My life hasn't been this exciting for months, year's maybe! It's like competing in a never ending adrenalin adventure sport. Average on any level doesn't exist here. My senses are permanently heightened, loving every single moment when I'm up and feeling so incredibly worthless and pointless and angry when I'm not.

At this very moment it's a beautiful life. People are smiling, feeding me, being happy. And such wonder it's exposing! Last week I'd no notion that I'd be here, today. And likewise, what follows tonight is as yet all delightfully hidden. An ever changing odyssey, a festival of fascinating newness (it may not be good but 'new' is a fair second best) that until now has been shamefully taken for granted.

Swallows catch insects late afternoon. The sun is powerful still, all-consuming, like a tomb, my shorts stick to the sheets. A magpie hops up to the window – locked open to an inch only to prevent us all jumping for merciful release - to inspect the human. I marvel at the way it accepts me in one glance. Beyond it the trees lean over the Pentagon, shading the swarming, depressed masses. Medway's so green! Have I been blind, not to notice this?! What a sky, such colour, hazy pale blue.

"John, John, can you see those swallows swoop…?"

The chattering gossips of the night shift drone on until daybreak. Minutes later, it seems, although it's in fact seven – I've dozed – I'm woken by

"David Wise?" It's the blood lady. She checks my wristband to ensure she's got the right patient and waits for me to mumble an agreement. She wants to make sure I'm awake so that I can feel the pain.

"A little scratch,' she smiles and jabs the needle into my right arm, "or a nasty sting, whatever you like to call it…"

Wise, David, 680222BF, my wristband reads, meaning, that the first David Wise admitted here would have been A, and then the second, AA, and I'm way down the list, at BF. There are so many of me here in Medway! Thirty two in all! Another sign of my un-uniqueness, if I needed convincing (I mostly don't).

The blue machine standing guard beside my bed bleeps and whirs round the clock. It sounds like a sea front arcade game vying for the crowds' attention with tales of heart beats and oxygen levels. Sixty six in one box, ninety eight in the other. That's me, the digits, the wavy line, the maths grid. I'm reduced – perhaps have never been anything else but - a mathematical equation. One of a trillion. The drugs pull me under until dusk.

Reg, the old giant whose voice sings of hop-fields and springtime, rouses me with his sobs. The pulse box reads fifty four. He cries as he talks to his wife. Despite her death fifteen years ago she's still a dab hand at wiping away his tears as she listens to all the things he should've said whilst she was breathing.

Do I have ten years, thirty, fifty, or more? Reg is me. What to do, though, in-between my bed and his.

The days fade into one. There's little to separate them. Occasionally an alarm sounds, signalling that somewhere in the ward a life is undecided – go or stay? Nurses run, rubber soles slapping on lino. My finger glows red as the monitor traces my heartbeat, racing now. Sixty, sixty six, seventy six, eighty eight, one hundred and ten…the metal strips that'd fixed the ECG leads in place, now hanging loose on my shoulders, flap and wave like worms in the rain, rhythmically responding to the blood thumping beneath them.

The doctors, a huddle of corduroy and crumpled white linen that shuffles the length of the ward every morning, can tell me nothing, for fear of being sued if they get it wrong. They speak as if my health is not my business, but purely the concern of a hundred-grand-a-year consultant (later I learn that they rate my chances of survival at one in four).

"I'm going to leave your spleen in," says the head man, "let's see if it can't recover. You're a unique case, you've a fractured rib, a ruptured spleen, and heavy internal bleeding…you should've lost your spleen immediately. And the period when you lay in the car, after the blindness, well, let's just say you're very lucky to be here…" After he leaves his assistant sits on my bed, strokes my hand and whispers

"If it were up to me, I'd have the spleen out, save you all this pain, I'm very sorry…"

Despite their disagreements about methods of treatment I'm certain that all the staff are doing their best for me. Regardless though, mostly I'm an unhelpful, argumentative patient. I'm not dealing well with the rapid transformation from athletic travel writer, in training to run his first marathon in Sri Lanka, to somebody who can't even walk to the toilet.

My wavy line settles into a flat calm.

"My hearts stopped," I think, "but I feel ok, have I…? Whilst dozing? With the minimum of fuss? Have I passed on? In my sleep? Well, thank goodness all that cruelty and sadness is all over with…"

Then the line flicks up mountains again, and a nurse is pouring tepid tap water into a scratched plastic beaker.

"Drink more, you must," she urges, "have you evacuated your bowels yet today?" I haven't but I nod assertively because I want her praise. "You have? Keep on like that and you'll be home very soon…"

Existence is brought down to the basics here. Gone are the everyday questions like

"Who am I?"

"How did the universe begin?"

"How does my brain work?" And other recipes for destruction and instead its

"Have you eaten?"

"Have you drunk?" and

"Have you been to toilet?"

The nurses ask twice a day what my drug chart says. They can't read the doctors' writing. I don't blame them. It's an illegible scrawl. A university education and these doctors can't even communicate adequately. Ten percent of NHS hospital deaths are down to errors brought on by not being able to read drug charts and notes. Why can't they – whoever 'they' are - introduce a rule that demands easily understandable BLOCK

CAPITALS from everybody who works in hospitals?

My scan results aren't good. I've a larger haematoma sitting on my spleen than first thought. Four and a half centimetres in length. A kindly doctor says, off the record, that this can mean that I'm getting slightly better and that the blood clot is dispersing, or alternatively that the people who did the first scans weren't very good and didn't measure my clot properly. Either way, he concludes, I won't be going home anytime soon.

I can hardly accept that I'm human, less still that my body is me. Look at this feeble wreck! And yet, inside, I feel so very alive. It seems idiotic at this moment to pretend that the spirit cannot exist independently of the body. I begin to comprehend what I heard (felt?) in those African rainforests, the inaudible voices, spirits clinging to trees now the flesh and muscle has decayed…

I snap at a nurse who are you to keep me alive? What is it you're trying to preserve? Look outside, all of you! Walk down Chatham High Street. See how we treat each other; see what vile creatures we are. What is it exactly you're trying to preserve?!! I hate myself for hating them and apologise immediately, recognising my own madness, my irrationality, my clouded mind.

The painkillers pull me into halfway land. I daydream of the things that my friends and I will do after we're free of these stupid bodies. All is white again, the voices hum, speaking myriad languages, surrounding and comforting. I drift into focus occasionally, hear tired relatives talking to incoherent patients, pronouncing words roundly and slowly like children, not waiting for any response.

The changes that were never made…if only…if only I hadn't been so immature, that time on Brighton Pier, or beside the sheep wash at midnight, if only I'd believed that what I said and did actually mattered, and was master of what came out of my own mouth.

At what point did this become inevitable? When did I cross the no-going-back line? I'm not alone in thinking this, I'm sure. Tonight the ward echoes with sobs as people reflect on their lives. An alarm sounds; we listen intently for the direction of the footsteps, to figure out in what room the Reaper's at work. If only…

for a second chance! I think; what a life I'd make of it!

How stupid I was, not realising what I was getting into, and now, the slow realisation that I may not be getting better as quickly as I'd hoped, that I lay here and life is in the balance, that inside me my spleen is struggling to keep itself together. That life, if it continues, may be changed for ever.

"I evacuated my bowels in a plane toilet over New Delhi," Laurie says. He's very specific about location. "Right over the city itself. I warned them I had stomach pain, but they just ignored me, so I soiled my pants, and stuffed them into the toilet bin, and somehow the smell infiltrated the plane's air condition system…"

"Oh God, oh dear," moans Reg.

"Not my fault though was it," Laurie defends against nobody but himself, who's still battling with the awfulness of the incident, "it's obviously the airlines' for not helping me when I first said I had stomach pain." He breaks off with a massive fart. Nobody laughs, verbally slaps him on the back, or acknowledges what he's done. It's OK for sick people here to do anything they want. I've learnt that lesson very quickly. I sink in my dreams, drowning. All is peaceful.

Another needle, left arm punctured this time, bloodstained sheets – the doctor looks surprised as he withdraws and blood spurts out, what did he expect? - and it's Sunday so there're no clean ones to be had until laundry gets going again sometime Monday. The fragile body, so susceptible to little knocks, and how it needs to be fed! I hate to rely on such a faulty mechanism. It's like driving a donkey and cart when really your brain needs a F1 beast.

Laurie's flying on morphine. He reclines in his chair, feet up on bed, slicked back grey hair shining, backlit with reflected light bouncing through the window.

"Take anything you want," he slurs after John asks for a pen, "help yourself to it all."

The first time I had bad pain - it kicked in with the blindness - I was too horrified and scared to notice what was actually going on. I couldn't observe myself. But today I'm calm and can savour it. I've refused my medication and am able to receive pain lucidly. I feel the needles sliding under the skin, probing, the fluids pulsing into me, a little colder than my blood. The whirring CT scanner, shuddering, then iodine squirting into my arms, lighting up my veins and lungs, a warm burn starting in my neck and racing to my groin.

"It feels like you're wee-ing, right?" the consultant says. I politely agree with him, although it doesn't feel like that at all, rather like when I see a real pretty girl and there's a rush of blood, a primal blush.

Tom is the sixth inhabitant of our room.

"Oh Tom, you poo-ed your bed again," a nurse says.

"Mmm, maltesers," her helper jokes and then catches a whiff and wretches. Tom chuckles behind his huge round spectacles like a naughty little boy. He's huddled in the foetus position, as he is everyday, confused and incoherent, looking like a cartoon tortoise, wrinkly, slow, ancient, a motionless skeleton…

 The days blend even more. I can't tell anything except that I'm still bloated, if I shave and wash I feel better, and that whenever I return from the toilet a nurse will approach me with a clipboard and ask if I have 'evacuated'.

I wake to hear Karen mouthing off foreigners.

"They're all like that, tight," she finishes. She's ranting about the Philippine nurse who just refused to hand over more drugs than were needed. This gentle British racism, this institutionalised bigotry, the result of not having to cultivate her views (a relatively harmless activity in one but murderous in a group), infects her as deeply as does her tumour.

A Polish nurse is shaving Tom. Laurie demands a bed bath.

"Can't you do it yourself? Are you in pain?" she asks, "I know you English, you never let on if you hurt… the stiff upper lip, yes, stiff…"

"Can't let the natives see you're hurt…" says Laurie bashfully. Here comes the flag again...

England. England.

Oh, for an Englishman worthy of the title! What use would they be though, in this day and age... but everything is snatched conversation. Received between bouts of floaty emptiness. My room-mates may also be saying great, wonderful things. Yet I switch off from that, so angry am I today with myself, with all humans. I want nothing to get in the way of my contempt for the species.

After my daily toilet excursion, where I strain and puff and then confront my ravaged reflection with

"Hold on, don't go, for what is love without you?" I sit on the edge of my bed, gathering my breath, looking straight at Tom. His eyes flicker, see there's nobody else around...he whispers

"Please...please?" The man he used to be, and still is inside, is speaking. Reaching out to me because those nearest can't hear what he really wants to say any more. He frowns and holds out his hands, looking despairingly at the drip feed. I think he wants to die. Because what is this life that he leads, this being spoon fed and bed bathed and messing his bed all day, and staring listlessly into open space the rest of the time, and being spoken to as a baby, when really he's a man.

It's Sunday, my second here. I look with envy as everybody gets served a roast beef dinner. This is my ninth food-free day. I'm dizzy, even without the painkillers.

The nurses banter happily, I hate them for smiling when I feel so low. I have no information. My hand throbs, the canula spike is immense. My arms are sore and bored from being punctured so often. I feel like I'm climbing a litany of false summits. The dye the CT man injected me with this morning, the iodine, and the vile potion I had to drink to highlight my organs, give me the runs. I'm camped out in the toilet for hours with violent watery spasms.

There's much activity around Toms' bed all night. Doctors' too-ing and fro-ing and muttering. A strong smell of poo lingers for an hour or so. There's no wind to blow it away. I pull the covers over my head, not wanting to breathe the germs in.

I'm allowed a meal. Later a sharp pain seeps across my lower abdomen. Perhaps it's the food, reanimating my intestines from their ten day slumber, or a bit of blood blister breaking free from my spleen and making its way out. I crunch up, eyes widening, slope to the toilet, hoping to poo it out, whatever it is, sit there touching my toes, trying to ease the passing, but nothing comes, not even wind. So back to bed, where the nurses are washing the floor in my bay. My belongings are piled up and there's no place for me to sit, I feel the colour draining from my head. I lay for the rest of the day after they finish.

Visiting time. I'm sweating on top of my sheets. The ward's full of lethargic creatures in ill-fitting sports clothing and badly bleached hair that begin every sentence with

"I'm not being funny but…" or

"to be honest…" or

"at the end of the day…" and end it with

"know what I mean?"

Question and response. No thinking, just reporting, repeating lines heard on TV or radio, but rarely, if ever, in the heart. A nation of kids aspiring to a vocabulary of less than a hundred and fifty words just so's they can measure up to their peers and football heroes.

Peter's guests - an old lady, a young boy and a man - settle and talk the normal inane, comforting rubbish. Nobody notices the young boy messing around with the catheter until Peter starts moaning, and then the boy is shaking the tube like a garden hose, watering his dad and grandma as if they're roses (weeds?).

Three emaciated lions adorn the majority of breasts, white feathers in their manes. One time symbols of honour, bravery and integrity are now the heralds of cowardice, betrayal and base stupidity. Or perhaps time has just shown them for what they truly are and have ever been. Elsewhere the children of the enlightenment read their Voltaire, scoff at the British yobs and then remove their mask with a drunken elitist comment (or not drunken - worse). The individual sees, the crowd stumbles.

Laurie dresses for home. There's little that can be done for him. He's eighty-one and the cancer is well advanced. He must die in comfort among his own family. There's a delay with his drugs coming up from pharmacy, a good three hours late, so he misses the ambulance that was going to give him a lift. He lives twenty miles away.

The next day he has his drugs and is ready for the ambulance. Two butch spiky haired women in green jumpsuits arrive to collect him.

"You can only take one bag," they snap in unison, pointing at his three plastic carriers.

"But I've been in here three weeks; I needed a few changes of pyjamas, what am I supposed to do with them now?"

"It's the rules," they shrug, "there's no room for any more. Your family have to collect them later."

"My wife doesn't drive, and my son's in Australia. I can put them all on my lap."

"Only one bag," they insist.

"I'm not leaving them here."

"Then we can't take you." They waddle away, and Laurie prepares for another night in hospital.

The sun sets to the left of the war memorial. Strood is rimmed in gold, its terraced windows shimmer. My last sunset? It's sounds dramatic, but, whoever knows, so I'm glued to the glass, aching from the falling globe, a symphony of colour, art as good as it gets. Behind me wee splashes the floor as another catheter fails. John's stomach gurgles, a nurse passes with two two-litre jugs full of strawberry cordial coloured wee, the monument slices the sun in two, grey clouds blush crimson, rays spike out from the concrete lollipop, the globe is racing now, the overcrowded towns glow; it's not beautiful at all down there, no, no! The whole world is mine, I don't have to care about this place, I can lower my roots elsewhere, my brain calls the shots, not sentimentality; I want to go home.

"I've a fear," John confides, "that I'm being chased, that I have to do everything now, before…it catches me up."

"I know," I agree, "I feel the same. It's got its hands all over me right now. I feel this pressure on my neck when I sleep. Pressing my head right down into the mattress so's I can't breathe."

"Sometimes," he lowers his voice, "I feel like, well, it'd be better to stop whilst I'm ahead, you know, the whole picture becomes clear, and you see what the future is, and it's not as good as the past, better to slip away before you become a burden…"

"I think that too when I'm down. But when I'm up anything can happen..."

"Perhaps." Silence. Emptiness.

"That should be a terrace really, full of flowers," I say, stirred by a crow pecking at the flat roof outside our window, "what's the first thing you'll do, if you get out?"

"Swim with dolphins," he brightens at the thought. "And you?"

"I'll plan a big Medway festival. Have lots of fun. Spend all my money. Its crap lying here knowing I've got a bit in the bank. So I'll spend it all, help myself to forget that living is utterly pointless and boring." John laughs

"God bless our trinkets…"

I lay, drained totally, staring at the ceiling. The biggest challenge that any human faces is in convincing themselves that all this matters enough to motivate the urge to take part happily. That birth and death is not just separated by a great expanse of boredom that can never be extinguished, only glossed over with gimmicks, like twinkly lights hung above a babies cradle, no different from TV or music or art or sport or work. All time filling attention grabbers.

Laurie moans over breakfast about the bolshy ambulance drivers. A nurse says a complaint is being made against them. Reg wee's his bed after morning tea and accuses a nurse of taking his watch. It's found under his sheets, a little damp. Then he packs his bag and gets a taxi back to the care home.

Another scan today. The stomach pain's increased. My heart and blood pressure monitoring machine purrs, snores, like a cat. I could sleep along to its rhythmic beat if it didn't insist on tightening on my arm every hour and waking me.

"The scan results aren't as good as we'd hoped," a doctor says, "so no food tonight, just in case we have to operate tomorrow." A 'Nil By Mouth' sign hangs from my lampshade. I hate it. Another cannula is stuck in my arm just before lights out. I feel like…like you would if you had needles stuck in both arms.

"Have you read this book?" I ask John, "It's about Mallory and Irvine climbing Everest." He shakes his head. "Irvine was so lucky. He just curled up in the snow near the summit and fell asleep. What a way to go."

"Lucky bloke. He's lucky allright." His stomach is gurgling very loudly and he moves with a grimace as he talks. He doesn't complain though – never does - I admire him for that, for his ability to suffer in rational silence.

"Imagine, just going to sleep and never waking up. How much better is that than this? Knowing exactly what you were doing. Maybe drinking a few scotches to set you off on your way. And such a view. Fresh air in your lungs."

"Yeah…falling asleep eh…my kids, you know, the wife doesn't let them visit too often, it upsets them so…"

We think this now, in here, but sure enough when (if) we get out, give us a few weeks and we would've forgotten this conversation, these sights and smells, the anguish and the cries at night from inmates, fellow patients, the fear of loss, that creates that chasm, that looks so un-leapable for us alone, we'll black them out…but how preferable it would be, the fresh air, the saying goodbye in such full spirits and clearness of mind…

Not that I'm clear of mind right now. That's what hospital is doing to me. The various doctors, each with their differing views of what's going on, and I, paranoid, thinking that rarely is it that things are done for my personal benefit, rather than as a guinea pig, but what silliness, to imagine myself of any importance, and so I sit in the sweltering heat, planning my escape. Thinking it better to discharge myself that to rot here, when really to rot here is probably what's best for me.

The pharmacist stands at the end of my bed, a six foot five African with a thick accent. Ghanaian, or Kenyan, maybe. It's like I've been in the desert for a month, and suddenly seen an oasis. Its not him, he could be the next Harold Shipman for all I know, its just the fond memories that he stirs in me, of Africa, of my time there, the freedom, the feeling of being at home. He asks the standard questions, did I take medication before I came in; am I really going to be put on a long course of antibiotics? No I say, just over the counter hay fever stuff, and my spleens still with me, so no antibiotics yet please. He moves on, talks to a new guy, Peter, next to me. Peter's very polite, then after the pharmacist leaves, he says

"Why'd he close the curtains, I couldn't see him!" and the bloke next to him, Andy says,

"Bloody niggers," and they both laugh.

England, England.

Peter calls his wife and gives her the bad news. He finishes with

"I love you." He never says that when she visits. But love, actually, is all around us - it always is when fear threatens to overwhelm.

The nurses are being especially kind to John. That's a terrible sign. If they're overly worried about you, you know you're buggered. He's got a blood transfusion into one arm and a saline drip into the other. The ward stinks of the poo that seeps gradually into his bedside bag. He sits, head lolling to his chin, eyes glazed, arms at his side, palms facing outwards (like a photo of a dead gorilla I once saw which'd been propped up for a hunters' prize photo) with his gown slackly limp across his thighs, his penis hanging out. He's done a remarkable job of shouldering physical dignity and sickness at the same time - either is a heavy enough burden on its own for most of us - but now it's too much. The nurses approach him, pulling rubber gloves on with a slap and swish his curtains shut.

More needles, more injections, more pills from an unknown hand. I feel like I've lost control. I've no say on what is put into me, what drugs I take, what course of action is next. I've been here so long familiarity's set in on their part. I hate this. I want to have a say in how I die. I hate the nurses for their smiles and happy banter. They've totally blown their chances of any Quality Street if I ever get out of here.

I wake to see John being sick, heavily, projectile red vomit, blood in via the arm last night, out via the mouth today. He sprays the wall and floor with an immense wave. The hole in his stomach gurgles and spurts even more fluid up like a geyser.

"I'm sorry for the mess," he gasps as the nurses try to stem the bleeding. To me he is nothing less than a God. His heroic defiance in the face of his own impending death, his refusal to sink into pity, is on a level with Scott's 'I do this to show…' note. I watch an Englishman being wheeled away. It's not good for us to see this, they say.

On the contrary, I think, it's essential to realise what's coming to us all. So that if we make it out of here, we live what remains of our lives as best we can, Kings in our freedom. As John is, as Reg is, so must I be. One day.

The desk fan that was cooling John whirs on, chopping up emptiness. His blood pressure machine is silent.

I slip from the ward, sad, hobble the length of the empty, sterile corridor, waiting for the shout - that means a nurse has seen me - which never comes, and head outside for some fresh air. I settle on a shady bench in front of the hospital. A group of fat women and skinny men, all doused in England football shirts and tattoos, one with a closed eye, smashed in last night by the looks of it, gather around a girl who's feinted on the lawn. I shudder at the sight of them. They panic like children as their efforts to revive the girl (which involve shaking her limp head and shouting "C'mon San', for fucks sake, c'mon,") fail. Behind us another man with blood trickling from a head wound onto his England shirt screams at a car

"Fuck off, I told you, you cunt, fuck off," and staggers off up the roadway, flexing his lats like a bats' wings, looking very satisfied to have caused such drama.

My new CT scan results arrive. The rent in my spleen is now six and a half centimetres long. How on earth could trying to do the right thing come to this? There's my naivety yet again; there're no rules, no boundaries, no right or wrong, it's just as it is. You are where you are. Wherever that is, that's where it is.

Some questions can never be answered, but need asking all the same. What *is* it that I'm preserving? What am I? Take away my name, my address, my job, then what am I but a string of relationships that will one day break. Families, friends, lovers. I abhor the idea of life being pre-ordained, that we have a story, a common myth, a heroes journey to complete to feel fulfilled, like a character out of Star Wars or the Wizard of Oz. Dogs bark, birds cheep, humans need to face up to fear and defeat evil, they say. Well, I'll leave that to the others, if I get out of here, I'll try to rise above that, and just be, and not attempt to find false comfort in my 'natural' inclination. I want to push it further. Push what? It. Me. It.

"Stalin considered this the first ever socialist novel," says the tea lady, the quiet one of the two, not the one with big bouffant hair who calls everybody 'lovey', the other one, as she flicks through my copy of 'Robinson Crusoe'.

"Really?" I'm dazed.

"Yes, that's what Malraux said anyhow. I love these plates, I've got a book at home, 'The Water Babies,' that's got colour plates in it like these…"

Her words take me up among the clouds. It's not that she knows of Stalin or Malraux that's so pleasing, but that she feels able to talk about them freely to me. Here, in North Kent, where knowledge of anything other than oversized gold jewellery and cheap cider is considered with suspicion and hostility, she's dared to learn about mad Russians and daredevil Frenchmen and more…she dares to talk of them.

England! England!

The Gods briefly show their munificence in the face of this Gentlelady.

A grey haired man arrives to occupy John's bay. The nurses mutter; I can only make out the word 'MRSA'. He's an upright, immaculate, distant civil servant type. He places a silver foil packet of sandwiches on his table.

"I won't eat hospital food," he says proudly to anybody who'll listen.

Six hours later he's on his knees before God. Back now from surgery he's struggling within the confines of an oxygen mask. Unable to get to the toilet, unsure of using the bottle, he calls the nurse. She advises him to sit up straighter,

"It will pass easier."

"I'm going to be sick," he blurts. His arrogance flows onto his sheets. Those of us who've been here a while know the procedure, and make ready to witness the funeral of his immortality.

Now he's begging God for mercy, for life. He thinks the pain is unbearable, that nobodies ever hurt like this before, whilst the fact is, everybody hurts EXACTLY like he does, that he's just another piece of meat occupying that particular bed, until the time comes when he'll move on, to the new world or back to this. That he's not the centre of life, that he's just one of a billion or ten.

He pleads meekly for a cup of tea. Thanks the nurse profusely. Momentarily, he's broken. He's a nice human being. Polite, thankful. Maybe he'll remember this when he's healthy again. Maybe he'll remember that he's at his best when he realises he's alone. Maybe.

For those with eyes to see, a serious illness is a prophetic vision of the future. The fit will only be helpless twice in life. Once as a child, which they'll have little memory of, and secondly as a pensioner, when it'll be a time of no more second chances. But this sickness lark, when you're once again helpless, when strangers bathe you, soothe your brow, wipe your bum, clean up your mess, feed you, keep you alive, this is a shot across the bows, saying, live whilst you can! Do everything you want whilst you are able! What an ability I have, or will have, I'm sure, soon - I can walk, almost, talk, live independently of machines, eat what I like, go where I like, I can do anything!

A new admission, fresh from surgery, stands besides his bed sobbing.

"I'm peeing nurse," he says, "but it's coming down the sides, not the middle." He stands there, just wee-ing, its splishes onto the lino. He's distraught, can't work out what's happening to him. That his body is old and broken, and he's now wee-ing out of some rent that's appeared near the top of his penis. He's scared and so are many others in here because, because, there are no answers.

When his wife (a trim, well manicured woman who from behind looks half her fifty-odd years) arrives, he uses her as a sounding board, reporting all the things that he's told the nurses, who've been negligent, as have the doctors. In reality, he's said nothing to the nurses of the sort, and why should he have, they've been marvellous to him, as they are to us all. But he needs to assert his authority over himself, needs to regain control, let off some steam, become once more a man. She nods, yes, agrees with him, how slack the NHS is, if only they'd gone private, they could afford to, didn't he know that? What have they been saving for all this time? All these years of scrimping! He waves her away with a weary self-sacrificing grimace. No, the savings are for the new house, the holiday, for the kids, he doesn't want to waste it on himself. What a man! The wife hugs his arm and looks worried. How the kids will get it in the ear later! What sacrifices we make for you! And do you appreciate it? She spreads a cold towel over his forehead. He drops off to sleep. She leaves, heading for a sleepless night created by his macho, weak lies.

If this were a novel we patients might have fine words in our mouths. Humour, insight, wisdom. But there's none of this. Just silence, and what's needed to get what we want, and careless phrases borne of anger directed outwards - towards nurses who regardless of our rudeness continue to do their very best for us - because we're uneducated, and unimaginative, and therefore can't comprehend how we deserve what is happening, can't realise that this is how life is. That we're not important, no more than an insect in Patagonia or Bhutan five thousand years ago was, and that it's all…nothing personal.

An old lady is wheeled in. She begins to moan. Then yell. She thrashes and screams behind her drawn curtains. There's a constant 'beep-beep', like a machine has become unplugged. The nurses don't come to turn it off. They left as soon as they'd put the breaks on her bed. It's a particularly rude night shift tonight. I can hear them in the reception area, just a few metres away from the lady's bay.

"D'you know," one says, "Marge reckons that nine out of ten Africans in her clinic are HIV positive! And that two out of three that come to our country have Aids!"

"I just don't know why we let them in," adds an Asian nurse, "bloody immigrants."

Come on England, Come on England.

The lady yells in tongues, no language that I can discern. I go to the toilet and try to peek at her but it's too dark to see anything through the crack in her curtain. I wonder what part of the world she comes from and if it's better there than here. She seems to settle, but then, having drifted a little, I'm woken again by her near-inhuman shrieks. It's three thirty am. More 'beep-beeps'. Her saline tube's probably come adrift. She thrashes about for half an hour. The heavy air is full of huffs and thumping of pillows and "fuckin 'ells". Nobody wants to curse the lady, but we need to sleep. I'm dog tired, I don't want to hear this pain; I want to get better, not be constantly reminded that I'm in the morgue's waiting room. I run my fingers over my face. Feel all the dry skin and scabs on my forehead that weren't there when I came in. It's due to the bad water, a nurse said yesterday, bad water, here in a hospital. And we're meant to be getting better. I look like a leper. I flip onto my front, my comfort position, catch my canula on the metal grid headboard, yelp.

After breakfast a consultant tries to talk to the old lady.

"Its no use, she only speaks Polish," explains the staff nurse.

"Can we get an interpreter in?"

"We'll try." The lady spits out a tirade of incomprehensible anguish.

"Can we move her to a side room?" the consultant raises his voice above hers.

"We wanted to keep her under close observation," says nurse.

"But she's ninety one for God's sake," the consultant huffs, rather too loudly, more for us patients than the nurse or his fellow doctors, "she's allowed to die."

"But Mr J-, there's a pile of paperwork if that happens."

"What's this world coming to," the consultant mutters.

She looks frail. Old even for her advanced years. She can't speak a word of English, doesn't know what's happening to her, has no known relatives; just what is it the nurses are trying to preserve? Life isn't sacred, not at all. But what matter these thoughts, this is the way it is sometimes, and there's no stopping it. The most one can hope is that death will be quick, and perhaps, pleasant, shared with familiar faces, not drawn out and welcomed in by strangers from a strange land. Whatever our misfortunes with our sleepless night, they're nothing compared to the panic and pain she's feeling right now. But do I feel guilty for cursing her nocturnal screams? No, of course not, I'm human, a fallible, selfish creature by nature, a bit of meat where all roads, all lines of thought and communication, lead to me.

The nightshift gossip like they're in a wine bar. The new nineteen year old lad with a swaggering cockney manner chats up the married blonde, who keeps giggling, whenever she gets something wrong

"Well, I *am* blonde…" They talk of theme parks and Big Brother and other banal stuff because they're bored and they're skirting the real issue like secretary birds dancing around each other, some elaborate mating ballet based not, though, on evolution, but on repression. It keeps me awake. The blonde repeats three times

"Me cars so old the only thing that works is the door 'andle," followed by a giggle. Everybody laughs. Poor people, they must be so bored. A mobile phone rings and sounds like a buzzing fly. It's very annoying.

The same nurses I curse now tomorrow I praise, it's not they who fail, in particular, it's my moods, stuck here, peeling in this bad air and bad water place, my vanity increasing with each layer of red flaky skin shed. My moods make my judgement suspect; all of those nurses, even the very worst, do the job a hundred per cent better than I would care to do.

The Polish lady cries murder when the nurses try to change her gown. I see her for the first time, a shrivelled prune of a thing, a stick-thin-Auschwitz survivor look-alike, pointy jutting chin, incredibly wrinkly, but sharp eyed, still there…the cries are not of madness, but perhaps of surprise, and of the childlike inability to withstand the least pain that seems to afflict humans at times. I stand and stare, and listen, ignoring the lure of the radio, the many charts and announcements on posters that litter the walls for our information and distraction, and when I eventually tear myself away from the sight, which is difficult, like leaving the scene of a car crash whilst it's still being cleared up, I concern myself with the future, and what I'm to do with myself. It's terribly difficult to work that out.

England play Portugal in the World Cup. The day-room that hosts the TV is full and sweaty. I stick to the seat, the back of my clothes damp. Men sit clutching their colostomy bags. I pray for a boring game, lest fists punch the air and wee goes flying. My wish is granted.

I ask when a doctor will be round; I want to know when my next scan is.

"There're only three doctors on call, and they only see the serious cases," says the nurse. I thought as much. I'm decaying here, but not seriously enough to be seen. I get their point, but now is the time, surely, just let me go home and see how I do. Stay here any more and my face will fall off, my legs will waste away, and I'll catch some horrific long term illness from one of these sick people. A new one just got wheeled in. Dementia, advanced, won't accept medicine, heavily sedated.

He's called John. Another one. In the future hospitals will be full of Kylies and Chantelles and Jades. John stinks badly of poo. He laughs and talks to himself. Won't move up the bed when he's asked. Doesn't want to stay in bed in fact. He's old and he's dying and he's confused, so he's up and down, not knowing where to go because every door bar one is locked to him now and he just has to slip away as best he can. The nurses call him darling, and flatter him as they would a baby, how shiny his skin is, they say, how strong his arms, squeezing the flimsy sticks that protrude from the skeleton. God, how necessary, yet how horrible, is this, to be old and treated like this, this false flattery, which is well meant but false all the same, spoken to as if he were never a man, never did all the things that no doubt he's done.

"Lie down John," a nurse says, "take care of yourself, you're confused, you've got a drip, you'll knock it out if you keep on, stay still," and I don't care at all, all I know is it's hot here, in my corner, and I'm stir-crazy and can't wait till Monday and the scan result that will allow me home.

John has a visitor. An old lady. Happy, making the best of things. She's been doing this for a while, I think, learning how to make the best. Admirable. This is sometimes how love goes. I'll do all in my power never to let anybody have to tend me like this. John is dying. I can smell it. It's not poo now. Different. Musty, very personal to him. This is the smell of Johns' death. I don't want it near me. I'm frightened of it. No doubt if I reach his bed it'll be my smell too, although with a personal slant. Maybe baked beans, or curry, in with it.

I enter the halfway zone, courtesy of painkillers, all is white and hot and floating disembodied voices. Belgium is full of paedophiles, somebody says, more than any other place on earth, according to an independent study. Daniel O'Donnell is a genius. It's hospital radio. I raise myself, decide to put a stop to the love songs (painful! Every one of them illuminate the seething black hole I've glossed over), and phone in a request.

"Hotel California and Won't Get Fooled Again." Together the tracks represent a full fifteen minutes or so respite from the utter rubbish that usually gets played.

"Who's that second one by?"

"The Who."

"Can you spell that?"

"W. H. O. And try to play the entire keyboard and drum solo please."

Just as 'The Who' begin the nurse arrives to take my blood pressure. She's concerned about my heart rate. Up from sixty four-ish to the mid nineties.

"I'm listening to Keith Moon," I say by way of explanation.

"I come back very soon, next hour," she replies. They cut the song at the start of the drum solo then switch the focus of the request program to Shelley Ward, where all the mentally ill people are. The requests come in for Mariah Carey and some awful rap songs, as you might expect.

Today's' blood test got mislaid. Or messed up. Whatever, I have to have another.

"You've got very good veins," says the young doctor brandishing the needle.

"Yes, they've been very popular recently." Despite my veins' obvious charms, they're missed yet again, and the needle wiggles its way for some few seconds before it strikes home.

I return from my nightly bathroom routine. Poo, shower, clean teeth. Draw my curtains. Think that this isn't *that* unpleasant. I have my little corner. Two metres by three. Separated from all by two blue, green and yellow patterned curtains. I also have a cupboard on wheels. With two drawers. One for chocolate and cake (well stocked) and the other for clothes - shoes, trousers, shirt and socks. On top is piled everything else that I need for life here; soap, flannel, razor, towel, shampoo, toothbrush and toothpaste. A trolley holds a water jug, a cup, two books and a pot to wee in. And out there, on reception, a softly spoken nurse, chattering happily to her friends in a language I can't fathom but enjoy the music of, who'll tomorrow bring me medicine and breakfast in bed, and all my other meals in bed if I need her too. I have everything I need. Yes, tonight I am fond of this prison, these sandy caramel walls, this green lino, these starched white sheets, these oxygen tubes and lamps on arms, reaching over me like protective aliens.

The nightshift gossips about the tramp in the next ward who got set on fire recently by rich boarding school-kids in Rochester. He's had to have both his legs amputated, but still he managed to go missing yesterday. Apparently he wheeled himself as far as Woolworths in Gillingham, a mile away, before being caught. They laugh at him. Secretly admire his freedom, perhaps. Beggars are the only choosers. The only ones not scared of loosing what they've got (because they've got nothing), the little life-rafts (obstacles?) made of houses and nest-eggs and partners and admiration and flesh and blood.

I'm overcome with fear for no rational reason. I just can't believe that I'll make it to daybreak in order to go for the scan that'll set me free. I'm exhausted, and overcome with an oppressive feeling that I think of as the hand of death, just squeezing all resistance from me. I know that I've been lucky, and I can't help but think, why me, why have I been let off like this?

I'm afraid to sleep. I'm obsessed with the notion that I'll not wake up. Despite my frequent words to the contrary, I don't want to die. I hold Robinson Crusoe in my hand, so that when I drop off it'll hit the floor and wake me up. But then I reason, this way madness lies, I need rest, sleep, and I can't go on like this, fearing the dark, when I might fall without control, no hand on the brake should I feel things turning badly, so I lay on my back, staring at the dark, feeling very frightened, alone and unimportant.

Finally, here's the realisation. I must try to accept this fact, this solitary unimportance, and not be scared. Just a little more time, I find myself whispering, I've so much to do still. If I can just be spared for a few more years, like a character in 'The Iceman Cometh', no doubt…

I'm surprised to wake up. I'm still here. I didn't expect to be. This is not overly dramatic. I've felt how my body is when I'm nearly dead, and this is it. This can't last though. I must come to the point where I believe I can get better, instead of just hoping to exist until daybreak.

The consultant says there's been a mix-up, that I can't have my scan as promised. I have to stay in hospital another week, perhaps. I've been here three already. I can't stay any more. I've got cabin-fever and I fear for my life. Hospitals' a great place when you really need it but the better you get the more of a risk you run by staying in. MRSA's always on the horizon, leading an army of unknowns against any needle puncture, any weak spot. I collect my belongings amid heartfelt offerings of

"We do our best, you know," and discharge myself.

At home I hobble round the sitting room, a room I thought I knew so well yet am visiting now for what seems like the first time. Touching things. Plants. Videos. Candle holders. Books. Thinking back to when I bought them, or to who gave them to me, looking at them in a more interested, generous light. Crying because the beauty of my experiences and friends, which comes to me with each memory, is too much to take. This could really be the last time I see you, old thing, Conrad, Chatwin, Thesiger, Haggard, Doestoyevsky. 'The World of Suzi Wong', what fine memories I have of reading you in Hong Kong, and then wandering Wanchai afterwards, looking for Suzi…I've always been stuck in the past, me. Yearning for the old days of honesty, beauty and honour. The days that perhaps never existed, outside the minds of the romantic, the naïve and the stupid.

England. England.

Then, in the freezer, a tub of double chocolate ice cream, oh yes, let me say goodbye to you my lovely. How fine you are. Aha, a bottle of Malawi gin! Let us converse closely tonight, my dear. Both of you, all of you, I want you all, not a moment to waste.

I feel so happy right now, happier than since childhood, playing outside during the non-stop sunshine of the '76 school holiday. It's so beautiful to be aware that time is limited yet of so sound a mind and body as to realise the value of what I'm leaving. Each object, each person. I feel so intimate with it all, there's hardly any gap between me and the trees and animals and indeed other humans, now that the belief in ambition and immortality has truly faded.

I morph into everything I come across, and am infected with urgency, telling myself, Come on! Just do it, whatever you want, eat that bit of extra cake, drink that whiskey, spend that money, yes, just do it, whatever you want, with whoever you want, whilst you can, relish this time before the next depression hits, or the hand tightens it's grip, enjoy the sparkly merry go round…

The police telephone. They say that the attackers haven't been found. Even though I was assaulted in the open space outside the Maidstone gaol, train station and central Post Office, there's no CCTV in the area. And the many human witnesses have all decided that they saw nothing.

"It's very frustrating, we'd love to get them, you must be very angry…"

"Not really, I don't know, maybe…"

"You're very forgiving, I wouldn't be, I'd want them to pay…"

Before, in hospital, early in the journey, there was deceitful pleasure to be gained from 'graceful forgiveness'.

"Those poor yobs," I'd say, "how terrible their lives must be," knowing that others would think well of me for saying so, offering me the confusion of, have I forgiven for real, or just the accolade? Is this a golden chance, I'd consider, that I've grasped fully? 'I'm beaten in body, but courageous in spirit, generous and positive!' Pah! Until I wanted to smash all the faces in sight! That is, to rid my world of surplus.

But I'm different now, and the police are wrong, as I was. What I feel isn't forgiveness. I have to live here, among these people. It'd be nice to be able to make the idiots leave Kent, leave England in fact, but, how would that work? Our island would empty as surely as if the Pied Piper had swept through. Hardly anything would function. We need the idiots; they're our bankers, our bakers, our printers, our insurance clerks, our families and our friends.

So, I move forward, I try to forget it all, and succeed mostly, except when my shoulder feels like it has a dart stuck in the front of it and I know my stomach is bleeding again and I have to take things easy. Then I remember, and I curse my bad luck. But hate? No. What's the point in expending all that emotion on people like that? I don't wish to hurt them either. Since I've left hospital I've developed an extreme aversion to aggression of any type, verbal or physical. The mere hint of a threat throws a steel wall across my soul, leaving the speaker dead to me. For a sane man there's no victory to be had in seeing somebody quivering before your fist. The only winners in violence are the losers. And I don't want to win, because to win somebody's got to loose. No, the worst I hope for my attackers is what they already have; a lifetime spent with themselves.

My spleen now has an eleven centimetre gash across it, the doctor says, but the sun is shining and I want, need, to get outside. I should be resting, but this is what I do, and my demise is ultimately all of my own making. I feel better, another crest presents itself for conquering, then the pain comes, and I'm swept to the bottom of the hill again. I take a tentative walk through town, England flags deck most windows and chests, it's like a Nuremberg rally, a prelude to a frightening, sinister future, then onwards up Sturla Road, a steep slog, I have to hold myself back, as I can't let my heart rate race, lest the fragile spleen be flooded with blood, so I walk hunched over, slowly, like an old man, and the kids playing football in the street jeer, laughing at a failing body. If they knew that I once walked continents with my world in my backpack, would their laughs turn to respect? No, what does it matter anyway, this is what it comes to.

I bury my head and walk away, as quickly as I can. I feel so powerless since the assault. What can you do if you're attacked in England nowadays? Your choices are to get beaten up and suffer a complete lifestyle change or, if violence is your way, to fight back and risk imprisonment for assault. And if your attackers are under sixteen, which is increasingly likely, it's even worse. You either take the indignity, the kicks and the promise of death, or you fight and get labelled by the police and the media a child-beater.

Sympathy is wearing thin. I've been out of hospital a month now. I look much better, my friends say. Have more colour in my cheeks. I break contact with them because I feel so ashamed of what I was. I don't know why, I just want to forget all of the past, all of it, including them. In return for my ignorance they say, in private,

"He's laying it on a bit thick now, isn't he?"

I take part in a re-construction of the assault for a BBC program in Tunbridge Wells. At one point I'm lying on the ground with three men, all amateur actors, around me pretending to kick and punch. They're very convincing - one receives a bloody nose from a flailing elbow. The cameraman's hidden away, low down beside a car, trying to get a wide angle shot. On two occasions women walk past, see me getting a beating, don't clock the cameraman, and quickly turn away. I don't expect them to intervene, but it'd be nice to think they might call the police. Later, we call the police ourselves, and ask if anybody has reported the violence. No, the officer says, they've had no calls that morning.

England. England.

I don't feel part of this England any more. This is not my country, not my life. The yobs rule the streets and the tabloids whilst the cleverly-spoken liberals protest from the safety of garden parties, radio four talk shows and broad-sheet internet chat rooms and are too gutless to even use their mobiles to summon help for strangers in distress. And then there's me, and people like me, or are they any others? I feel so outnumbered and surrounded right now, but there's me, and I can't move, my right to do good has been confiscated. The police aren't concerned with morals, merely with upholding the law - a law which so often comes down in favour of the attacker and not the victim - and recognising the need not to breach anybodies human rights, even if their subject's busy abusing those of others.

Political correctness and worse still, media correctness, decides our minds for us, making our speeches for us, with both eyes ignoring all but the most perfunctory of truths, fixed solely on tomorrow's newspaper headlines. 'Universal truth' is an oxymoron but personal truth...if we could just recognise some of that we could strike a blow against division, because nothing separates us more than individual natures that are based and moulded on a collective mistake.

But I'm dreaming. The fact is I've lost control of everything and it's all (my opinions, my reliability, my sanity) gone to hell. Or rather, I've realised that I never had any control over anything in the first place.

I can't walk the streets of Medway because the least bit of physical contact, even the average busy, self-absorbed Westerner knocking me with shopping bags, will send me back to hospital and perhaps to the morgue. I can't exist in the outside world as it stands. I'm awash in this godless fatherland, my set of outdated rules trampled by contradiction. I feel that nothing I do, no business created, no community action raised, no friendships forged, will be worth it, for what force would stand up to save my efforts from being washed away and forgotten, or soiled by, them, them, and I have absolutely no power here in the modern world and nothing to keep them at bay, with their eloquence to explain away, to justify.

I should come to terms with all this if I want to feel better. Face my new place in this new world head on. But I've neither the spirit, the energy nor the intelligence to do so just now. So instead I work out a simple diversionary tactic, an easier option. I dig out my pinhole camera, join the National Trust, and bury my head in a sand concocted of castles, stately homes, small villages, good manners, scenic countryside and…the past.

The past is controllable and safe. I can pick and choose my scenarios and my outcomes. I begin to spend my days looking for the old haunts of yesterdays' great humans. Mostly I settle myself in areas where famed writers have brushed the earth, and read their books in-situ (which adds not so much to the texts as to the places). I find these books to be solid, comforting and complete companions. They're human, minus the spur of the moment impulse that leads to wrong action, word and thought. They're not real portraits of people, time and place. Why would they want to be, when they can be so much more?

They can't touch me here, they, everybody, the vulgar modern age, when I retreat into history, when I take refuge behind Virginia Woolfs' broad shoulders. The years strip the media yob explanations of their gloss and leave only the lies, bare for us to see, and for a few hours a day I'm safe and happy, no longer doubting myself, and in my new strength I see a future, honestly built and maintained, impervious to the shadows of men blinded by the glint of gold and self-advancement.

In my dimension the villains get their just rewards, love rules. Everything is not for the best in the best of all possible worlds. It's more than that. Everything is as it should be. I choose realms where good wins. Where communities are tight knit and aims laudable. I ignore the truths that are ugly, the despots, the criminals, and focus on snatches that please me. History, my edited version of history, is my anchor.

I tramp over Box Hill with Jane Austin, promenade parterre's with just and wise kings, picnic on French Fancies and Jammy Dodgers with ladies and knights, scribble my notes in a castle or a cottage by the sea, and with great painters and thinkers I delight in forgetting what I've learned, remembering what I know, then forgetting what I know and remembering what I feel…

They ignore the slime clinging to me, residue of my crawling through the sticky membrane of time, and offer the food of romantics – unconditional, polite acceptance. We dine in the still-point of moral annihilation, the eye of the whirlwind,

"This is enlightenment," says Conrad one morning, "if such a thing exists."

My pinhole camera helpfully ignores many aspects of the modern world of which I don't wish to be reminded. Busy roads empty and blossom, the cars moving too fast for my slow exposure times. People become wispy ghosts. Detail, colour and a sense of obviousness are gone, leaving only mystery and beauty. The pointless void regains some interest.

*****

The Gallery

I didn't think about doing anything with the photographs as I was taking them. The object was not to show anybody, just do them, and to enjoy the act. Which I did. The idea for this collection came months later, very recently, when I felt a need to draw a tangible sense of finality under my experience, and making them into a book seemed as good as way as any to achieve that.

Lacock Abbey, Wiltshire

Photogaphy was invented by Willian Henry Fox Talbot at Lacock Abbey in the summer of 1835. His first photograph, a pinhole, was taken with exactly the same sort of camera as I use (no lens, viewfinder, exposure meter or film—everything is guess work and the image is burned onto squares of photographic paper), was of the oriel window in the south gallery. My own pinholes show the window itself from the outside (in the left hand photograph it's on the right of the image above the door).

Lacock Abbey, Wiltshire

Lacock Abbey, Wiltshire

The abbey and nearby village have been used as locations in the TV and Film productions of 'Pride And Prejudice', 'Moll Flanders', 'Emma', 'The Mayor Of Casterbridge' and most recently 'Harry Potter' - the Abbey's **Cloisters** (above) and side rooms were transformed into the classrooms at Hogwarts School.

Lacock Abbey, Wiltshire

The **Octagonal Tower** (left) was added in 1539 after the Dissolution. Fox Talbot and his wife are buried near the Abbey in the **Village Churchyard** (right).

Monks' House, East Sussex

Virginia Woolf said of Monk's House in 1930 that "It contains a large room where we sit, eat, play the gramaphone, prop our feet up on the side of the fire and read endless books." The house echoes with American voices; somebody proclaims loudly how lovely everything is. I have to agree. I walk through an orchard laden with rosy life, sit outside Virginia's **Writing Studio** (left), read the first chapter of 'To The Lighthouse', and think (for a second actually believe, and am comforted), how wonderful, I'm not alone.

Petworth House & Park, West Sussex

The largest herd of fallow deer in England are scattered over the hills, sheltering from the oppressive sun. I settle under a huge oak, whose great branches spread up and out and then down to rest upon the grass many metres away. It's cool under here and I see no sign of humans, apart from the very visible hand of Capability Brown. I'd walk more but I've exerted too much today, exploring this vast park and then the house, lingering too long in front of its many Turner's, so instead I slump back against the bark, feeling the blood seeping

into my stomach, and worry that I'm slowly fading, and think of the time in the car, the feeling of solitude, of being helpless, of hearing other cars going by, and then hospital...that's how it'll be in the end. There'll be the idle chat of nurses, trying to keep my spirits up, and their own also, and the tinkle of the drugs trolley as it makes its round, perhaps another cup of tea poured by a volunteer, and then that'll be that, and there'll be no more for me, and how very sad that is, because life is so good, here, now, this sunlight and these trees and deer, and its terrible to think it might end, even though it has too.

Abinger (left), Surrey and **Coleman's Hatch** (right), East Sussex

E.M. Forster moved to Abinger in 1924, the year 'Passage To India' was published. He lived there for more than twenty years, during which time he wrote 'Abinger Harvest' and 'An Evening Walk Round By The Yew-Wood On The Pilgrims Way'. Coleman's Hatch in the Ashdown Forest was home to W.B. Yeats and Ezra Pound for three winters (1913 - 1916) whilst Pound was acting as Yeats' secretary.

Brighton

It's another stunningly hot September day. I take in the **Pier** (left), where Hale is murdered by Pinkie in Graham Greene's 'Brighton Rock', then Madeira Drive, then pass through the average sites of a 21st century British town - pound shops, buffet restaurants and clubs and pubs offering cheap drink promotions - to the **Royal Pavilion** (right), which King George IV spent thirty five years and a fortune transforming from the 'farmhouse' he rented in 1786 to the Eastern style palace it is now.

Brighton

In 'Vanity Fair' W.M. Thackeray describes Brighton on the eve of the Battle of Waterloo as "Brisk, gay and gaudy, like a harlequin's jacket". Whenever he stayed there it was at the **Old Ship Hotel** (right). Charles Dickens wrote 'Dombey And Son' whilst staying in Brighton. He also lodged at the Old Ship.

Brighton
Chichester Terrace (right) in Kemptown, the setting in Dickens' 'Dombey And Son' for Dr Blimber's 'hothouse'. Nearby is Sussex Square, where Lewis Carroll lodged.

Brighton

Jane Austin writes in 'Pride and Prejudice' that "A visit to Brighton comprised every possibility of earthly happiness" for her character Lydia.

Sheffield Park Gardens, East Sussex

It's easy, when walking in such gardens, to understand why humans once worshipped trees. Two huge powerful individuals rule over the main lakeside. High and wide and with many thick branches soaring out of their thick trunks. Majestic Gods. Red lilies cover a smaller lake. Coots pace over their pads, testing them quickly before each step. Their young try to keep up but fall in short of almost every pad before struggling on. Ducks peck at my pinhole changing bag, looking for bread.

Wakehurst Place (left) West Sussex, a stately home and garden run and maintained by the Royal Botanic Gardens, Kew, and **Chiddingstone Village** (right), Kent.

Standen, West Sussex
A family house full of the work of William Morris and other Arts & Crafts designers.

A. A. Milne, the creator of Pooh Bear and Christopher Robin, lived at Cotchfield Farm near Hartfield in the Ashdown Forest. "Pooh's forest and Ashdown forest are identical" said Milne's son in his book 'The Enchanted Places'. Poohsticks Bridge is still signposted from a carpark, as is **'The Enchanted Place'** (left). General James Wolfe, the hero of Quebec in 1759, was born in Quebec House, Westerham, Kent. Pictured above right is the Quebec House stable.

Chartwell, Kent

The home of Winston Churchill. The views over the Weald of Kent, far reaching, the coolness at height, the lakes, it would be easy to believe in England, to fight to preserve it, if this is what you look at every day as you breakfast. Churchill was a gifted writer and was awarded the Nobel Prize for literature in 1953. In all he wrote fifty one books, including 'The History of the English Speaking Nations' and 'The History of World War 11'.

Chartwell (left) and **Ightham Mote** (right), Kent

Entrance to Chartwell House is by timed ticket only. I arrive at the ticket desk behind a group of German tourists. The clerk beckons me forward and says under his breath, "You're in first, at 11am, before this group of *Germans*." It could be a 1970's comedy sketch, except it's not comedy, it's real, and it wouldn't be very funny at all if I were in Germany and the situation were reversed.

Ightham Mote, Kent

Ightham is the moated tudor manor house dating from 1320 used by Anya Seton in the climax of her novel 'Green Darkness', where her heroine, Celia de Bobun, follows her priestly lover from Midhurst and is walled up in "The lovely and mysterious manor".

Ightham Mote, Kent

Knowle, Kent

Vita Sackville-West was born at Knowle house. She had written eight novels and five plays by the age of eighteen and later went on to write 'Pasenger to Teheran', 'Pepita', and the best-selling 'The Edwardians'. She was also the heroine of her lover Virginia Woolfs' book 'Orlando'. In one scene from the book the young duke Sebastian looks down from the Knowle rooftops "On a lawn of brilliant green" and hears the guests "Laughter and the tap of the croquet mallets". The croquet lawn is shown on the right.

Knowle, Kent

Sir Thomas Sackville, also of Knowle, co-wrote the early English drama 'Gorboduc'. Under other owners Knowle welcomed John Dryden, the first official poet laureate, in 1668. Sika and **Fallow deer** (right) still roam the surrounding park freely, as they have done since the days of Henry VIII.

London

Trafalgar Square, where George Orwell used to sleep rough and shave in the fountains, as recounted in 'Down And Out In London And Paris'.

Westminster, London

I bypass Westminster Abbey, where rest Chaucer, Drayton, Benn, Dickens, Shelley, Keats, the Brontes and all the rest and head for service at the Cathedral, the red and white striped church halfway to Victoria that looks like it should be in Cordoba, not Westminster. Dim lights fall out of the crypt arches, illuminating green marble pillars. The choral whirl is a highlight, I think, it's the one time in life that a strangers babies' cries sound truly miraculous, and now the call for blood and body, so I shuffle through the pungent incense,

not a patch on Jerusalem fog but plesant enough, and line up for some crisps, for some days they're the flesh of Christ and some days they're just crisps, and today they're just crisps. The cathedral is a third full, with an international flavour. As Arabian cripple hobbles away. London becomes human. He mumbles. Behind him the clergy bow to the crucifix, so large half is obscured by the gloom thrown down by the great dome. They file out, people shuffle, babies cry, their screeching horrible now the spell is broken. My head throbs, glows, from the sun and the wine.

St Pauls Cathedral, London

Tower Bridge, London

Drinking wine, sitting by the Thames, alongside others, all with wine, all with foreign accents, taking time to sit and admire, amazed and enlightened. A little high with a pinhole eye and man is good, the buildings magnificent. We laugh as the commuters rush by, coats flapping, mobile phone earpieces hidden. They are talking, shouting, crying, telling jokes, to nobody. Mad or very, very busy. Same thing.

Buckingham Palace, London

Bloomsbury, London

Russell Square (left), was mentioned in 'Vanity Fair' and was also home to William Cowper and Thomas Gray. **46 Gordon Square** (right) was Virginia Woolfs' first house in Bloomsbury. She described it as "The most beautiful, the most exciting, the most romantic place in the world". She also lived in Tavistock Square (as did Dickens) where she set up the Hogarth Press and which now has no sign of Virginia save a small bust in the corner of a leafy square crowded with lunch-time drinkers.

The British Musem (left) and **The Strand** (right), **London**

G.B. Shaw wrote his first play at the British Museum, whilst Keats gained inspiration for his 'Ode On A Grecian Urn'. The museum library has hosted Lenin, Marx (who worked on 'Das Capital' here), Engels, George Eliot, Robert Browning and H.G. Wells among others. The museum guards ignore the hoards of schoolkids clambering over the pillars, shouting, scattering rubbish and instead ask me to take my tripod down and go inside to apply for a pinhole permit, of which they'll have none. I decline their offer and leave.

Kensington, London
Beatrix Potter often sat drawing in **The Natural History Museum** (left) and a large collection of her paintings are held in the nearby **Victoria and Albert Museum** (right), which is also the place to go to view some of William Morris' best books and designs.

Kensington, London

J. M. Barrie walked every day in Kensington Gardens, and it was by the **Round Pond** (left) that he met the Llewelyn-Davies boys, who inspired him to write Peter Pan. The **statue of Pan** (right), near the Long Water in the gardens, appeared overnight in 1912 because Barrie wanted children to believe it came there by magic.

Kensington, London
The Royal Albert Hall (left) and the Albert Memorial (right).

Oscar Wilde lived at **34 Tite Street** (left) in Chelsea, where he wrote all his major plays. He would often stroll north to Picadilly, passing **Horseguards Parade** (right) on his way...

...as well as **The Mall** (left) and the statue of **Captain James Cook** (right).

The **Statue of Eros, Picadilly Circus** (left) and a **side-street** just beyond Albany (right), the exclusive address where Lord Byron, J. B. Priestley and Graham Green all had rooms at various times.

Chelsea, London

Thomas Carlyle made his home in Cheyne Row (left) from 1834 until 1882. His house (right) is kept as he left it. In those days it was considered that the Carlyle's lived in near poverty. It's a four-story town house, and one which I would call luxurious, a stones throw from the Thames. It shows what was considered poor by the days' writing elite, they must have had high standards. George Eliot lived nearby, at 4 Cheyne Walk, as did D. G. Rossetti and Swinburne (number 16), whilst Hilaire Belloc was at 104.

Chelsea, London
Carlyle Mansions (above) has been the home of T. S. Eliot, Henry James and Ian Fleming. Fleming wrote his first James Bond novel, 'Casino Royale' here, partly based on his experiences of wartime naval intelligence work.

Hampstead, London

I walk from **Wentworth Place** (right), the home of John Keats (a brilliant poet who sold only a few hundred books in his short lifetime), the place where he fell in love with Fanny Brawne and where he wrote 'Ode To A Nightingale', past the house of George du Maurier, author and grandfather of Daphne, to **Fenton House** (left), a 17th century merchants house, full of early keyboard instruments and costumes that were used in the recent BBC production of 'Bleak House'.

The **Cathedral** (left) and **Long Hall** (right), Winchester, Hampshire
"I take a walk every day for an hour before dinner," John Keats wrote to Fanny Brawne in 1819, "under the trees, past the beautiful front of the cathedral". One day, after walking through the watermeadows, he composed 'To Autumn'. Jane Austin spent her last days in Winchester, and is buried in the cathedral.

Watership Down, Hampshire

Richard Adams set his story here and these pictures, taken just east of Sydmonton, show where, in the novel, the strange rabbit with ears "Shining with a faint, silver light" finds Hazel and helps him slip away, after his adventures are over, "Running easily down through the wood, where the first primroses where beginning to bloom".

Clouds Hill, Dorset

The **cottage** (left), the home of T. E. Lawrence (Lawrence of Arabia) from 1923 onwards, stands on the edge of Thomas Hardy's 'Egdon Heath', near Wool. Hardy soon became a favourite visitor of Lawrence's, along with G. B. Shaw and E. M. Forster, who considered Lawrence's first version of 'Seven Pillars' a masterpiece. Lawrence carved into the **lintel to the front door** (right) two words in Greek which, loosely translated, mean 'Why worry?'

Lawrence died whilst riding his motor bike in 1935 – accident or assassination is still the question, he was the Lady Diana of his day - along the **Bovington Road** (the left-hand photo shows the exact spot). Forster was too upset to attend the funeral, held at **Moreton Church** (right) although Winston Churchill, who wrote of 'Seven Pillars' "As a narrative of war and adventure it is unsurpassable", Siegfried Sassoon and many others did.

Lawrence is buried in a **simple grave** (left). A cat named Elsa lives at the grave. She's fed by an old lady with a black placid boxer dog, who watches peacefully as the lady puts out food and water for Elsa in a bowl that she retrieves from behind Lawrences' headstone. An effigy of Lawrence in Arab robes can be seen in **St Martins On-The-Wall Church** (right) in Wareham, the oldest church in Dorset. The warder is happy to explain to me the history of the the red paintings above the altar, which are reminiscent of those I've seen in Aland and Cappadocia.

Brockhampton, Dorset

I reach **Thomas Hardy's cottage** (left) via a un-logged fungus filled forest, enjoying the snorts of stags and rustles of squirrels, and scrump plums from the orchard over the fence from his garden. The cottage, where he was born and set parts of 'Under The Greenwood Tree', is very humble. Then to his **grave** (right) at Stinsford Church, where I think, all these graves I'm visiting, it's liberating! To think that people, whoever we are, all end up here, that we all share this same fate. So "Why worry", as Lawrence wrote, why worry.

In Thomas Hardy's book 'Tess Of The d'Urbervilles', Tess's homeless mother claims shelter at **Bere Regis Church** (left), Dorset, below the "d'Urberville memorial". Later in the book Tess is at at "Heathen temple", a location based on **Stonehenge** (right), Wiltshire, resting among the stones with Angel, listening "A long time to the wind among the pillars".

Stonehenge, Wiltshire
The site is packed with tourists, which my camera dutifully ignores - there's light cloud and exposure time is around forty-five seconds, so people don't register.

Bath

A very friendly city - countless pinhole photographs are ruined because people start to chat to me whilst I'm counting the exposure times so that I loose track and overexpose. Charles Dickens used the **Royal Crescent** (right) as the scene of the "Extraordinary calamity" suffered by Nathanial Winkle in 'The Posthumous Papers Of The Pickwick Club'. Jane Austin also used the Crescent as a setting, in her novel 'Persuassion' as the place where Anne and Captain Wentworth enjoy walks.

Bath

Jane Austin thought Bath allright, until she had to live there, when she developed a "Very determined, though very silent, disinclination" for the city. She ridiculed the cities "Stupid parties" full of people talking "Common-place nonsense" in her novel 'Northanger Abbey'.

Tyntesfield, North Somerset

I walk beside the tennis courts to the boating lake, then up to the great Gothic house, thinking how nice it is that people lived like this once, perhaps still do. It doesn't matter that it's not me who's got all the luxury, as long as somebody has, that they have a chance to have such a wonderful life, can spend their days playing tennis and eating cream teas and taking gin sundowners, should they want to.

Tyntesfield (left), North Somerset and **Silbury Hill** (right), Wiltshire

Glastonbury, Somerset

Climbing the Glastonbury Tor at 8am, the dew has just evaporated in great clouds of mist, below me the sheen that remains makes the fields glisten. I understand why some people think this land, Avalon, England, enchanted. Two people are at the summit, they keep their distance but smile if our paths cross, it's a small area, and I think that, yes, these isolated pockets of decency and wonder that make my land so miraculous, these islands of calm, this archipelago - almost submerged in greed and selfishness - this is my England.

Views from the summit of **Glastonbury Tor,** Somerset

Glastonbury, Somerset

Avebury, Wiltshire

The great stone circle at Avebury was built around 5,000 years ago. The majority of tourists I see today are stone huggers. Straggly kids are encouraged to touch the stones, their parents wander in a trance. My modern trickery, for that is what the pinhole seems to be viewed as, receives a few hostile glances. Perhaps they're warranted, for it's a modern luxury to reject pin sharp obvious photos, to have such a glut of them that I want only for fuzzy, timeless outlines.

Avebury Stones (left), Wiltshire and **Lulworth Cove** (right), Dorset

Durdle Door (and nearby beach), Dorset

Mist swirling like bonfire smoke encases me as I walk back to Lulworth from Durdle Door. I'm incensed by an official sign that reads 'No photography, filming or painting here for commercial purpose without permission!'. What a cheek! Who says who can paint where! Who really owns any piece of land! I expect such foolishness from city-dwellers, but for those influenced by the sea? Who can honestly sit quietly before Durdle Door, or any natural sight, and continue to believe that they somehow have authority over it!

Calne White Horse (left), Wiltshire and **Cowden House** (right), North Somerset

Corfe Castle, Dorset

An owl in my campsite's pine woods hoots. A man in the next tent barbeques as if he's cooking a roast at home. I'm quite happy to sit here naked in my tent drinking wine and eating peanuts. Does wine taste different in plastic cups? Only if you've got the forest removed from your heart. The birds say goodnight, I forget my injuries until I lie in one position for too long or look down whilst going to the loo and see my stomach, swollen and disfigured, and then I remember, and wish all manner of realisation on those boys...

Kingston Lacy, Devon
The National Trust's largest, working lowland estate.

Kingston Lacy Egyptian Sarchophagus (left) and **Main House** (right), Devon

A red spider has made his nest between the tent and a guide rope. His web shines beautifully under the full moon.

Batemans, East Sussex

Rujyard Kipling lived in this 17th century manor house from 1902 until his death in 1936. The bookcases, which I pore over, hold much religious text, which is strange, I think at first, for such a non religious man, until a steward explains that Kipling was meticulous in his attention to details in his stories and he used these books to research thoroughly. Kipling described finding the house in his autobiography,"We reached her down an enlarged rabbit-hole of a lane…at very first sight, we said 'That's her! The only she!'" He moved here from

'**The Elms**' in Rottingdean (above left), where he'd written 'Kim' and the 'Just So' stories. As I pinhole 'The Elms' the owners stare aggressively and stand, arms crossed impatiently, before their front gate, which is rather silly of them - what might they expect, moving into the former home of one of Britain's best loved writers, that no pilgrimages would be made?

Kiplings' daughter was the last person to live at **Wimpole Hall** (above right), near Cambridge. I enter the house to escape the intense midday heat, intending to stay only a

short while, as my camera is useless indoors, but such is the beauty of the decor that instead I float around for a good few hours. All rooms flow into each other tastefully, this is no standard museum as some of the National Trust houses are. The centrepiece, reached through any of four outer chambers, is a large circular sitting room with pale yellow walls, an immense fireplace, and a ceiling tapering into a central dome which reaches up through the house's three floors to the roof itself. I finally drag myself away and take more pinholes of the house's **south facade** (left) and the **parterre** (right).

Cambridge

I walk along a shady alley, towards Kings College, set up my tripod, a lady barks fiercely, "No tripods here, you have to have a permit!" I understand immediately that this is nothing to do with tripods, or me, so I take no offence. She feels powerless in todays world, I can see that she tutts over the TV news, moans that people aren't as they were. She needs to impose some manners, some rules, in her own way. I give her a chance to like me. "Ok, I didn't realise,' I say meekly. She takes no notice. "How did you get here?" "Along this alley."

"Well, you shouldn't be here." I point at a host of people walking by, most with shopping bags, she questions none of them at all. "I just saw all these people and thought it was ok to walk here, they all are…" "They've all got tickets." She's almost sneering now. Instead of taking my meekness as a sign of good manners and an opportunity to ease up on me, and enjoy our meeting, she sees it as a weakness, a way of spending frustration, so that she'll be able to go home this evening and say, "I gave them what for, the freeloaders, thinking they can take photos anywhere, with a tripod, can you imagine, a tripod!"

E.M. Forster, who was described by D. H. Lawrence as 'the last Englishman', studied at Kings college in 1897. A few years later Rupert Brooke, also a student at Kings, famously wrote

"If I should die, think only this of me:
That there's some corner of a Foreign field
That is forever England."

England; a concept, not a nation or a flag, a measure as to what good humans can aspire to, can achieve, conjured up at times when enough of us get desperate. Lost? No, it is not for us to loose. Perhaps sometime soon it will appear again. I pack up and leave. Get a distant photo of Kings over a cow field, then walk up a narrow road, with no pavements, which is crowded with Japanese tourists, who are urged aside by a fat middle aged chap peddling his bicycle furiously, ringing his bell and shouting "This is not a pavement!' when in fact it is neither pavement nor road, but both. He sounds very well spoken,

perhaps he works at one of the universities. I set up my tripod in the road, a public road, outside **Trinity** college (above right), the former home of such advanced souls as Francis Bacon, John Dryden, A. A. Milne, Lytton Strachey, Leonard Woolf, Edward Fitzgerald and Lord Byron, and a bowler hatted porter runs swiftly out of the front gate and orders me inside to sign a register. "This is private land here," he says, "we need to know you're not doing this for commerical reasons." "But it's a road," I say. "We own it," he replies. I pack up and leave. These people, do they really not understand, that they're links in the chain, and they can only abuse the other links for so long, before they break? The fat chap on the bike, the one abusing the Japanese tourists, would he jump at the chance of a university post at a Japanese college, or a well paid research assignment there? And then, should he accept, would he mind if he were bellowed at by an ill mannered oaf, for walking down the middle (for want of pavements) of a Kyoto road?

I'm asked several times about the camera, not in the usual interested manner, but with suspicion, as though the questioners, who are mostly young men, are plain clothes police.

"Why don't you use a digital," frowns one chap (probably a captain, or somebody higher, with that wit).

The roads heave with lads, healthy looking, ruddy cheeked, blue or white polo shirts, collars up, beige shorts, flip flops, dress down chic, talking loudly as they bowl three abreast over the cobbles and flagstones. Others lads shout through their floppy fringes, "Come and punt the river, river trips here…" Older men with clipped beards bike after young girls with floral dresses and shawls that blow off their shoulders. Oh those bikes! The riders whiz, bells ringing, their heads held erect, noses slightly upturned, never deigning to looked at those they scatter, those pedestrians, those vermin. The posture is perfect, they seem proud, ethically right on, no cars for them, on no, and no walking either, there's probably something wrong with going on foot, some way in which is destroys the ozone, or a monkey species in Arizona, or somewhere. Or perhaps it hurts them to leave the sanctuaries of their libraries, their laboratories, their colleges, and

venture into the real world, so they keep their eyes in the future, the dream, and not on those, those, those...pedestrians. It's terrible, actually, that here in Cambridge, a renowned centre of learning, that there is such a lack of visible intelligence. To think that somebody needs a tripod to take publication worthy photos, what ignorance, to shout at tourists just because they can't hear your silly little bell, what bad manners, to take out the frustrations of your own unhappy existence on those who haven't proved themselves worthy of your rants, how tragic.

Ickworth House (left) and **Melford Hall** (right), Suffolk

Aldeburgh, Suffolk

The pinholes above show the Moot Hall, built around 1520. It was the councils' meeting place for some four hundred years. Then it was positioned at the centre of the picturesque town but coastal erosion now means it stands only a stones throw from the sea. It was fully restored in 1854 when chimneys copied from Hampton Court were added. Now it's the meeting place of the Town Council.

Aldeburgh, Suffolk
Benjamin Britten (his grave is pictured above right, on the left of the pinhole) started the town's now famous annual music festival in 1948 not long after completing his opera 'Peter Grimes', which was based on a character created by local poet George Crabbe.

Aldeburgh, Suffolk
M. R. James used the beach near the Martello tower as a setting in his book 'A Warning To The Curious'.

Lavenham, Suffolk

Lavenham has been called "The most complete medieval town in Britain", a tribute to its fine collection of medieval and Tudor architecture. The older buildings are centred around the market place, with its 16th century **Guildhall** (above).

Lavenham, Suffolk

Dedham Village (left) and **Dedham Mill** (right, once owned by John Constable's father), Suffolk

Flatford, Suffolk

The Hay-Wain is a painting by John Constable that shows a scene at **Flatford** (right). Flatford Mill was owned by Constable's father and the **cottage** in the painting (left) belonged to a neighbour, Willy Lott, who was said to have been born in the house and never to have left it for more than four days in his lifetime. Willy Lott's house has survived to this day practically unaltered, but the water level is higher as this area of East Anglia has sunk into the sea by one foot since Constable's time.

Flatford Mill (left) and a nearby field where Constable used to walk, Suffolk

Flatford in winter, Suffolk

Bridge Cottage (left) and the scene of the Constable painting '**Boat Building At Flatford'** (right), Flatford, Suffolk

Views Of The River Stour between Flatford and Dedham, Suffolk.
The picture on the right shows the setting of the Constable painting 'The Leaping Horse'.

The River Stour (left) and the home of **Edward FitzGerald** (right), Suffolk
Edward FitzGerald translated the 11th-century Persian collection of verse 'The Rubaiyat Of Omar Khayyam'. One of my favourite sections of the original reads, literally,
"Before time takes you by surprise
Ask for good red wine and get wise
You are not of gold, don't believe the lies
You are put to dust, once again you'll rise."

Cavendish (left), Suffolk and **The Spread Eagle Inn** (right), Midhurst, Sussex
Hilaire Belloc, writer of 'Cautionary Tales For Children', loved to visit The Spread Eagle
Coaching Inn at Midhurst. H .G. Wells worked just up the road in the chemist's shop,
'Morton Hickson's', whilst studying at Midhurst Grammar School.

Uppark, West Sussex

H. G. Well's mother worked at Uppark below stairs, as housekeeper, in the 1880's. A certificate announcing Well's admittance to the local grammer school still sits on the kitchen sideboard. The house was later to become 'Bladesover' in Well's satirical novel 'Tono-Bungay'.

The White Horse Of Uffington (left), Berkshire, and **The Vyne** (right), Hampshire.
You can't see the White Horse from the ground. That's what everybody says as they walk over the fields up to its head. Not all of it anyway. It wasn't made to be viewed by man, I think, but for those who could get into the sky. I hear some visitors refute this when it's mentioned, it doesn't suit them to think of aliens or flying in the Stone age, or God. But the evidence is clear when you stand at its feet. The White Horse was not made to be viewed from the ground.

The Vyne (left), Hampshire and **Basildon Park,** (right), Berkshire
Basildon Park was used as a location (Netherfield Park) for the 2005 film 'Pride And Prejudice', and also as a filming location for the film 'Marie-Antoinette'. My favourite room is the shell room, where the owners' sea-shell collection is presented in cases and tall display units made from shells themselves. Upon inspection even the flower arangements that decorate the upper reaches of the room are fashioned from shells.

Basildon Park, Berkshire

Hughenden Manor (left) and **West Wycombe Park** (right), Buckinghamshire

The home of Benjamin Disraeli has a bad feel to it, created by just a few of the staff. It only takes one misguided fool to cast a dark shadow over any visit, and there is one indeed at Hughenden. A young girl scowls at me for no reason as I'm walking to the house, and then the receptionist ignores me, and although the older volunteers in the rooms are nice, it takes a while to get the sadness out of my system. I know its nothing personal, the girl probably just had to clear up the loo, or she's had a row with her boyfriend, or something like this

but...I expect such unaware behaviour in the street, people are often like that, but in a National Trust property? It would be nice to think not, although, this is my line in the sand, nobody else's.

West Wycombe Park (above) was the home of Sir Francis Dashwood, founder of The Hellfire Club.

Cliveden, Buckinghamshire

These gardens saw the first performance of 'Rule Britannia' in 1740. Later they became the home of the Astor family, who gathered prominent figures in the worlds' of art and politics into a group that was to become known as the 'Cliveden Set'.

Cliveden, Buckinghamshire

Claremont Landscape Gardens, Surrey

Claremont dates from 1715 and its creation and development involved some of the great names in garden history (Sir John Vanbrugh, William Kent and Capability Brown). Landscape Gardens first appeared as a general reaction against the formal planting of earlier fashion. They offered pleasant areas where people could walk in apparently natural surroundings, but which basically comprised of a series of carefully planned views. Each view was designed to evoke a different sensation, surprise, awe, melancholy, etc.

Clanden Park, Surrey

Burford Bridge Hotel (left) and the view from **Box Hill** (right), Surrey
John Keats stayed at the Burford Bridge Hotel in 1817, writing book four of 'Endymion' and 'In Drear-Knighted December' there. Three years earlier Jane Austin stayed a week with relatives at Great Bookham at the foot of Box Hill whilst working on 'Emma'. George Meredith, author of 'The Egoist', took in the view from the top of Box Hill every morning, sometimes accompanied by guests including R. L. Stevenson, J. M. Barrie and Henry James.

Polesden Lacy, Surrey

Whilst Jane Austin was staying at Great Bookham, just over the way at Polesden Lacy lived her friend, the playwright Richard Sheridan. According to a local paper, on October 10th, 1802, Sheridan entertained his tenants to "A grand harvest home...with true English cheer and ancient hospitality".

Polesden Lacy, Surrey

Polesden Lacy, Surrey

Polesden Lacy, (left) and **Leith Hill Tower** (right), Surrey

The **Independence Memorial** (left) and the **River Thames** (right) at Runnymede, Surrey

The High Street (left) and the **Statue Of General Gordon** (right), Gravesend, Kent
In Gravesend, foreigners need no 'Juden star'; they distinguish themselves with their very visible love of life, and happy family picnics by the Thames.

General Gordon of Khartoum lived in Gravesend during the construction of the **Thames Forts** (right), from 1865 to 1871. For these six years he devoted himself to the welfare of the towns 'poor boys', establishing a Sunday school in the **Mission House** (left) and providing food and clothes for them from his Army wage.

The Statue Of Pocahontas In St George's Churchyard (left), Gravesend, remembers the first Native American to visit England. Pocahontas sailed here with her English husband, was received at the court in London by Queen Anne, and, having become something of a celebrity, was 'taken up by society'. She died on board a boat at Gravesend in March 1617, before her homeward journey, and is buried in the parish churchyard of St George's. The exact location of her grave is unknown because the parish records were destroyed in a great fire in 1727.

The **Clocktower In Gravesend** (above and on the left of the previous page) was built in 1887, funded by public subscription to celebrate the 50th year of Queen Victoria's reign. The design of the tower is based on Westminster's Big Ben.

The Cathedral, Canterbury, Kent

The Cathedral was the destination for Geoffrey Chaucer's pilgims in his book 'The Canterbury Tales,' which has sold more copies than any other book bar 'The Bible'. It was also the start point of Patrick Leigh Fermor's epic four year walk from Canterbury to Constantinople, which he wrote about in 'A Time Of Gifts' and 'Budapest To The Iron Gates'.

Canterbury Backstreet (left) and the **Synagogue** (right), with a facade like a Pharonic temple. The backstreets are Canterbury's gem; the architecture and general feeling is fascinating and the people polite, not eyeing me up for my spending potential as is the case with those who swarm over the area nearer the Cathedral gate, where the only smiles and greetings come from foreign tourists.

Canterbury High Street (left), where the buildings stand firm but the crowds leave no trace bar a white blurry mist, and the **Norman Castle** (right).

Views Of The Stour River, Canterbury, Kent

Farm Scenes, Chilham, Kent

Chilham Village, Kent

Teston Cricket Ball Factory (left) and **Cranbrook High Street** (right), Kent
A policeman approaches a man loitering in the doorway of an Cranbrook Undertakers. "I'm the local policeman," he introduces himself, "can I help you?" How nice to have such a concept - a local policeman! Perhaps we should break all of our towns down into villages. Encourage more localness, more caring. I like Cranbrook, there's hardly a pair of too-tight hipsters with belly overhang in sight and everybody leaves me alone, whilst the few I choose to chat to are polite.

Cranbrook Windmill, built in 1814, the year before Waterloo. I share the site with an English couple and their French friends, who're very surprised to be walking around in sunshine, as England is *always* being rained on and they expected to be using their umbrellas every day. Of course, their English friends are chuffed to bits. "Yes, we have sun here, a lot, it's a lovely country…" The French were estatic yesterday, apparently, because the air was so clear in Dover that Calais were clearly visible, "We've only been away three days, but, we so miss our home…"

Tenterden Railway Station is nestled in an Age-Of-Steam time warp. Well used suitcases stand on the platform, piled on porters' sack barrows, a Pullman coach gleams in one siding - the polished crystal and silver and crisp white tableclothes visible through the windows - a dark green engine marked 'Ashford' in another. Squirrels and pidgeons raid a cobnut tree, dropping nuts onto car bonnets with a crack. A Penny Farthing bike is chained to shiny black iron railings.

Tenterden Railway Station, Kent

Tenterden Railway Station, Kent

Romney Marsh (left) and **Smallhythe Place** (right), East Sussex
Smallhythe Place dates from the early 16th century. It was originally the Port House when the village held a thriving shipyard industry but is now best known as the last home of Dame Ellen Terry, the great Shakespearian actress famously associated with G. B. Shaw, Henry Irving and the Lyceum Theatre.

Lamb House (left) and **High Street** (right), Rye, East Sussex

Henry James lived at Lamb House from 1898 until his death in 1916. Here he wrote 'The Wings Of The Dove', 'The Ambassadors' and 'The Golden Bowl'. He described the town as a "Haven on a hill top" and "A miniature Mont Saint-Michel". Lamb House now sports a portrait gallery of James' literary guests, which included E. M. Forster, Kipling, Hilaire Belloc, Rupert Brooke, Ford Madox Ford, H. G. Wells and Virginia Woolf.

Rye, East Sussex

St Mary In The Marsh (left) and **Camber Sands** (right), East Sussex.
Edith Nesbitt, author of 'The Treasure Seekers' and 'The Railway Children', is buried in St Mary Churchyard. The wooden memorial, visible in the bottom right foreground of the left photo, marks the grave. Noel Coward died with a copy of Nesbitt's 'The Enchanted Castle' by his bedside. He lived in the cottage next to the Star Inn opposite St Mary's Church, and in the graveyard he wrote, 'The Queen Was In Her Counting House'. He was said to have loved the marsh's "Lazy rivers, silvery green flatlands, huge skies and every changing clouds".

Lympne Church (left) and **View Over The Romney Marsh** from its graveyard (right), East Sussex

Appledore (left) and **Brenzett** (right) Churches, Romney Marsh, East Sussex
These and other Marsh churches were often used by smugglers to store contraband in the 18th century, as related in 'Dr Syn' by Russell Thorndyke. Brenzett church was also immortalised in the Edith Nesbitt ghost story 'Man-Sized In Marble'.

Joseph Conrad wrote two of my very favourite books, 'Lord Jim' and 'Heart Of Darkness', whilst living at Pent Farm, Postling, near Folkstone in Kent. He said of the view gained from a **nearby hill** (left) "This is the view I love best in the world.' Every day he would pay a visit to the **Drum Inn** (right) where he would swap sea-stories with the owner who was himself, like Conrad, an ex sailor.

Fields Near St Margarets (left) and **St Margarets Bay** (right), Kent

Ian Fleming, creator of James Bond, lived in a **small house** (left) beneath the cliffs in St Margarets Bay , Kent.

Sandwich, Kent, has the highest density of listed buildings of any town in England.

The Castle (left) and **The Fisherman's Beach** (right), Deal, Kent

The Beach (left) and a **Quayside Building** (right), Broadstairs, Kent

The Dickens House Museum (left) Broadstairs and **The Town Clock** (right), Margate, Kent
Charles Dickens called Broadstairs "Our English watering place" and praised the "Pretty little semi circular sweep of houses" and "First rate bathing machines". The Dickens House Museum is the house he described as Miss Betsy Trotwood's "Neat little cottage with cheerful bow windows" in 'David Copperfield'.

Backstreet In Old Town (left) and **The Tudor House** (right), Margate, Kent
George Bernard Shaw described Margate as "A dismal hole". I think it's allright, although the chips I ate for lunch were a bit tasteless (I reckon the oil hasn't been changed for ages) and the people are infected with that end of the world hopelessness that forces them to look only at each others shadows.

The Beach (left) and **The Port Building** (right), Margate, Kent

Karl Marx, author of 'Das Capital', visited the Royal Sea Bathing Hospital in Margate for help with his bottom boils. He had tried many methods to cure them, including hacking at them with a scapel, but had failed. The sea sorted him out, however, and after he felt better he walked the seventeen miles to Canterbury, which he described as "An ugly sort of medieval town…there is no poetry about it. Happily I was too tired and it was too late to look for the celebrated cathedral".

Margate Beach Looking Towards Reculver (left) and **Reculver Towers** (right), Kent

The Grave Of Dante Gabriel Rossetti (left), Birchington, and **Bathing Huts** (right) at Herne Bay, Kent

Rossetti, the founder of the pre-Raphaelitism brotherhood and writer of 'The Blessed Damozel', is buried at Birchington church. His cross was carved by artist Ford Madox Brown and Rossetti's sister, Christina, wrote a poem 'Birchington Churchyard' at the funeral. I take photos of the grave whilst teenage girls sit getting drunk, sprawled out on some graves behind me, talking loudly of sex, crying out to be noticed.

The **War Monument** (left) and the **Bandstand** (right), Herne Bay Sea Front, Kent

Bathing Huts (left), Herne Bay, and the **Harbour** (right), Whitstable, Kent

The Home Of Author Katherine May (left), author Of 'Ghosts & Their Uses', and a preserved **Boat On The Seafront** (right), Whitstable, Kent

Whitstable (left) and **Faversham Town Centre** (right), Kent

The Statue Of Thomas Waghorn (left) and **The Brook Theatre** (right) Chatham, Kent
Thomas Waghorn was born in Rochester in 1800. He opened up the Red Sea route and thus halved the time taken to ship goods between England and India. His statue is supposed to be pointing out the overland route to the east, but since this is geographically incorrect most assume he's just directing drunks (most of whom offer thanks by crowning him with a traffic cone or two) to Chatham Toilets, a few yards away under New Road Bridge.

The Command House Pub (left) and **The River Medway** (right), Chatham, Kent
The Command House Pub hosted the Urban Fox music, art and poetry gigs which revitalised
the Medway creative scene from 2004 to 2006.

The Home Of Authors' Charles Dickens And Zara Carpenter (left) and the nearby **Bandstand** (right, taken last winter, inspired by a pinhole I'd seen by Wolf Howard), Chatham, Kent

The War Memorial, Chatham, Kent

The War Memorials, Chatham, Kent

The Nags Head Pub (left), long time live music venue which has seen performances by such bands as The Milkshakes, The Long Weekend and The Len Price 3, and **The Castle** (right), Rochester, Kent

The Cathedral, Rochester, Kent

The Castle (left) and **The Corn Exchange** (right), Rochester, Kent
Both these buildings were featured in the work of Charles Dickens, for instance...
"'Magnificent ruin!' said Mr Snodgrass. 'Glorious Pile!' Echoed Mr Jingle, as the members of the Pickwick Club crossed Rochester Bridge and came in sight of the fine old castle."

And in 'The Seven Poor Travellers' Dickens describes the Corn Exchange "As if time carried on business there, and hung out his sign".

Eastgate House (left) was once the Dickens' Museum. Now the museum has been moved way out of town and the building is given over to a 'Regeneration' Committee. Dickens wrote his last words in his **Summer Chalet** (right) on the afternoon of 8th June, 1870. Not surprisingly, they were about Rochester…"A brilliant morning shines on the old city. Its antiquities and ruins are surpassingly beautiful, with a lusty ivy gleaming in the sun, and the rich trees waving in the balmy air. Changes of glorious light from moving boughs, songs of birds, scents from gardens, woods and fields…penetrate into the cathedral…"

Dickens described Rochester's **Guildhall** (left) in his novel 'Great Expectations' as that "Queer place…with higher pews in it than in a church", where Pip came to be registered as Jo Gargery's apprentice. In the same novel **Restoration House** (right) featured as Satis House, "With its seared brick walls, blocked windows and strong ivy, clasping even the stacks of the old chimney's…" Here lived the embittered bride Miss Havisham, and here Pip met with the cold Estella, with whom he fell in love.

The **Beach** (left) and **Cockham Wood Fort** (right), built to defend the River Medway in 1669, Upnor/Hoo, Kent

Cooling Castle and a **Cart** in its grounds, Isle of Grain, Kent

Dickens used **St James Churchyard** (above), Cooling, in the opening chapters of 'Great Expectations' as the setting for the books' central character Pips' first encounter with the escaped convict Magwitch. In the churchyard there are two rows of lozenge shaped stones marking the graves of thirteen children. Dickens includes them as those of Pip's departed brothers..."Five little stone lozenges, each about a foot and a half long, which were arranged in a row". The children died from malaria in the 18th Century and were from two families. None had lived for more than seventeen months.

St James Churchyard (left) and a **Cart** in farm grounds (right), Cooling, Kent

Fields near Cobham (left) and **The Leather Bottle Pub (right)**, Cobham, Kent

Dickens often walked with his father from their Chatham home through Shorne Woods to Cobham Hall park. He wrote "A delightful walk it was...through a deep and shady wood, cooled by the light wind which gently rustled the thick foliage, and enlivened by the songs of the birds". He visited the park the day before he died, as if to say goodbye. In the 'Leather Bottle' pub you can sit in Dickens' favourite chair, which he used whenever he dined there, and where, some customers say, they've seen his ghost return to.

Richard Dadd, painter of 'The Fairy Feller's Master Stroke' and 'Oberon and Titania', stabbed and killed his father at Cobham Woods before cleaning himself up in **The Ship Pub** (left) in Cobham and fleeing to France. He was later captured and sent to Broadmore.

Lord Tennyson stayed at Boxley, near Maidstone, when his sister married into a local family. He described **Boxley Church** (right) as a place where maidens "Pelt us in the porch with flowers".

Wat Tyler, the military leader of the 20,000 strong peasants revolt against the poll tax in 1381, freed John Ball, a preacher, from the dungeons of **Archbishops Palace** (left) in Maidstone, Kent in order to be the revolts' spiritual leader. Literary critic William Hazlitt, born in Mitre Lane, Maidstone in 1778, said "The English are rather a foul mouthed race" for whom "The least pain in our little finger gives us more concern and uneasiness than the destruction of millions of our fellow beings." Maybe it's time I gave my naive image of honour and decency another name?

My friend **Karl Farrer** sketching the Palace (left) as part of the 2006 'River Art' Project. Next to the palace stands All Saints Church, which contains a memorial to local man Lawrence Washington (ancestor of George Washington) whose family arms inspired the American 'Stars and Stripes' emblem. Marcus Samuel started the Shell company after his kids collected shells on Margate Beach and stuck them to a box, which he duely produced en-masse and sold for a great profit. His company grew rapidly after it invested in shipping, and his children were in time able to build a house in **Mote Park** (right), Maidstone.

The Samuels' house in **Mote Park** (left) in Maidstone, Kent, is now derelict and exudes sadness. Not far from Maidstone, near Elmsford, the hermit St Simeon lived inside a tree trunk for twenty years around the year 1200. His skull now resides at **The Carmelite Friary** (right) in Aylesford and his name lives on in that of many schools - 'St Simon's Stock' ('stock' being the old word for tree trunk).

The Friary, Aylesford, Kent

Farleigh Bridge (left), and **Stoneacre** (right), Maidstone, Kent

Stoneacre, the National Trust home of two male tenants in pink shirts (so obvious my dears!) who hover like store detectives, hating the fact that they have to suffer my presence. "Look at the hinge on that door," says one, "you won't find that in B&Q," as if I, a working class oik, must spend my days scouring the aisles of DIY stores. Of course, they jump at the chance to show me who's boss when I get my tripod out. A commotion ensues. I give in and balance the pinhole on a flowerpot as they glower suspiciously.

The Castle, Tonbridge, Kent

The Pantiles, Tunbridge Wells, Kent

I follow in the footsteps of William Makepeace Thackeray, Jeff Beck, Virginia Wade, Syd Vicious and 'Disgusted of Tunbridge Wells' and drink from the Chalybeate Spring, whose waters, which have a high iron content, are believed to have medicinal qualities. "Is this really good for you?" I ask the lad whose job it is to hand out mugs of the reddish water, hoping that he'll say "yes" and I can go home knowing I've done my spleen good today. "If you drink forty pints of it a day," he replies, "yes, it'll sort you out."

The Pantiles, Tunbridge Wells, Kent

Views of **Penshurst**, Kent

Sir Philip Sydney, leading poet of the 16th century and writer of 'Arcadia', was born nearby Penshurst Church at Penshurst Place. He died, having written the first great sonnet sequences in the English language, at the Battle of Zutphen in Holland.

Scotney Castle, Kent

The first time I visit Scotney the day is long and a little cloudy, so visitors are scarce. I circle the old mote, admiring the ruined house at its centre. Perfect reflections, powerful trees, and a mole inching blindly along the path, trying to burrow into tar, then woodchips, and tree roots, then snuffling off into the undergrowth towards the mote. I hope it smells the water before it burrows into that also. Such a smooth velvet coat, and huge hands, and little feet kicking against air as it burrows again and again and again...

Scotney Castle, Kent
The image on the right shows a detail of the tree of life cut into the base of a sundial.

Sissinghurst Castle, Kent
The home of Vita Sackville-West; her name is inlaid in blue tiles on the windowsill of the right-hand **Tower** (left), as you ascend to the first floor and her writing studio (where she finished 'All Passion Spent' as well as many gardening articles for 'The Observer').

Sissinghurst Castle, Kent

Sissinghurst Castle, Kent

In front of Vitas' **Summer Cottage** (right) there's a chair under a head of a lion. I overhear some tourists saying, "Oh look, the lion!" (even though it's too weathered to see what beast it really is), as though it's a significant item, perhaps mentioned in Vitas' writing (but I can find no evidence of this, either at the castle or on the internet afterwards).

Biddenden Vineyard (left) and **Chartham Village** (right and next page), Kent

The Biddenden vines trail away into a gulley before finishing at the base of a row of wispy blue poplars. The hum of chainsaws and tractor engine betrays the presense of workers down in the dip, pruning and gathering grape. The next field is empty of movement. A single barrel stands at the end of a row of green vine. The sun is uncomfortably warm, but just a minute in the shade and I'm shivering a mite. It's been four months since the attack yet the tennis ball feeling is still there, and I'm a little down about it. I know I should rest, but

every sunny day urges me on to make the most of it. I could chance it and say that there're going to be many more such days, but I've never been one to take such gambles, so I pray for rain tomorrow so that I may convince myself to stay in bed. And this pinhole project isn't helping! My retinas are sore from all this staring at the sun, trying to judge intensity and exposure times and how long I have until the clouds shift. I'll be like Axel Munthe if I'm not careful. Now there was a man with his head shoved in the sand! But what glorious visions that sand offered him, as it is me.

Bodium Castle, East Sussex

Bodium Castle, East Sussex

A **Martello Tower** (left) and **The White Cliffs** (right), Dover, Kent

If you enjoyed the Pinhole Photography in this book and would like to learn more about making and using a Pinhole Camera yourself...

David organises a variety of events throughout the year during which you can get to grips with the art of Pinhole Photography. They include days out in London and Southern England, weekends in Paris and Rome, and longer holidays to Greece and Egypt. All trips are suitable for total newcomers to photography. Please contact Urban Fox Press for full details of opportunities, dates and prices.

Website - www.urbanfoxpress.com
Email - info@urbanfoxpress.com
Telephone - 07989 776759
Mail - 6 Albert Road, Chatham, Kent, ME4 5PZ, UK

Also available from Urban Fox Press

Walking To Trafalgar

by David Wise

ISBN 0-9547374-9-0

A written and photograhic account of a journey through Andalusia, mainly by foot, en route for places associated with the Battle Of Trafalgar - Cadiz, Gibraltar and Cape Trafalgar itself - during the early part of 2005. Cover hand stamped.

Buy 'Walking To Trafalgar' or 'A Velvet Silence' by going online
to **www.urbanfoxpress.com/shop**
by calling/texting **07989 776759**
or by posting a cheque made out to 'Urban Fox Press' to us at
6 Albert Road, Chatham, Kent, ME4 5PZ, UK

Costs;
'Walking To Trafalgar' - Papercover £6.75.
'A Velvet Silence' - Papercover £12.50.
'A Velvet Silence' = Special Edition (in purpose-made linen bag, dyed red with earth from Mount Sinai, with a bag of spices from Cairo, a hand-printed pinhole photograph and a bookmark) £21.50.

Also available from Urban Fox Press

A Velvet Silence

Pinhole Photographs of Egypt and Israel by David Wise
ISBN 1 905522 11 8

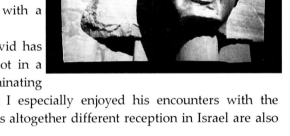

Review by 'Ancient Egypt' Magazine
"This is a fascinating, beautifully produced book, full of excellent *camera obscura* photographs, taken and developed by David en route. They transport the reader back a hundred years, whilst displaying the beauty and magic of Egypt's birthright with a panorama of dunes, fossil outcrops and oases.

   Much of the narrative is based on the dozen visits David has made to Egypt over the past years and whilst this is not in a continuous format, more in a diary style, there are illuminating concepts and impressions his experiences have yielded. I especially enjoyed his encounters with the emptiness of the desert and its peace. His comments on his altogether different reception in Israel are also intriguing and enlightening.

   The book's presentation is slick and the end papers are nicely produced from antique printing plates of an Arabic poem, translated at the beginning of the volume. The amount of work needed to produce this interesting publication has very obviously been a labour of love. One cannot fail to feel the passion of David's work, which manifests itself in every photographic plate. I found this truly gives another dimension to those of us who love and have journeyed into Egypt, whether as Egyptologist, holidaymaker or armchair traveller."

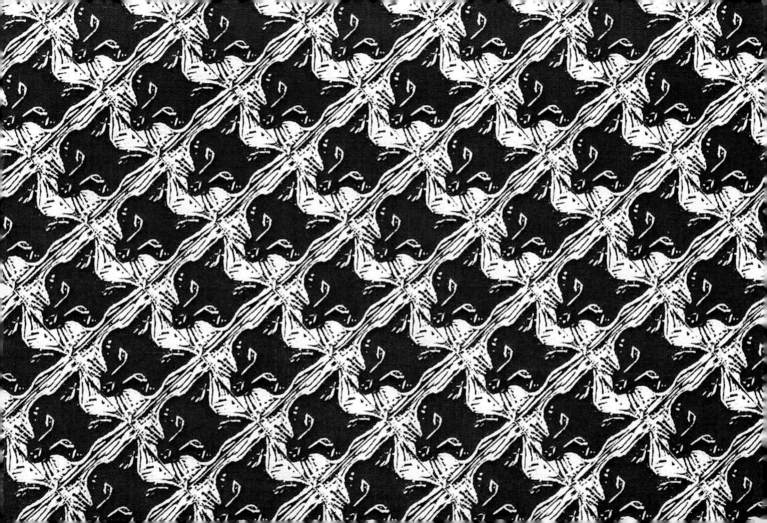

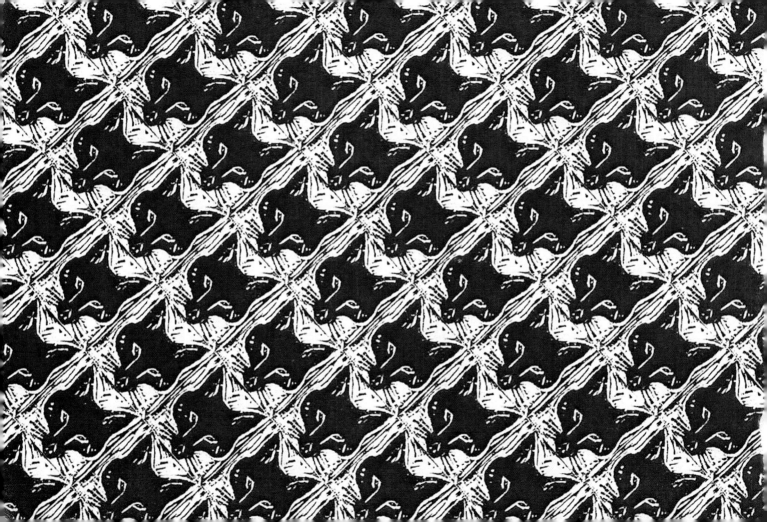